TROUBLED CHILDREN

A FRESH LOOK AT SCHOOL PHOBIA

Other books by the same Author

The Abuse of Care and Custody Orders and understanding
School Phobia (1989)

TROUBLED CHILDREN

A FRESH LOOK AT SCHOOL PHOBIA

Patricia Knox
B.Sc., Dip. Ed., Froebel Cert. of Educ.

First Published in 1988 by Patricia Knox ISBN 0 9512871 0 9

Second (Revised) edition in 1990 by
The Self Publishing Association Ltd
Lloyds Bank Chambers
Upton-upon-Severn, Worcs.

A MEMBER OF

in conjunction with
PATRICIA KNOX
Pen Llywenan, Bodedern,
Holyhead, Gwynedd,
N. Wales. LL65 4TS

British Library Cataloguing in Publication Data
Knox, Patricia 1937-
    Troubled Children : a fresh look at school phobia.-Rev. ed.
    1. Children. School Phobia
    I. Title
    371.295

ISBN 1 85421 106 4 pbk
ISBN 1 85421 105 6 hbk

Designed and Produced by the Self Publishing Association Ltd
Printed and Bound in Great Britain by Billing & Sons Ltd, Worcester

Dedicated to the memory of the boy I have called 'John' who died at the age of 24.

"I make myself - uninvited - a spokesman for children in this matter because they have so few other spokesmen and are in so poor a position to speak for themselves."
'Escape from childhood' - John Holt.

Contents

Acknowledgements

The idea for this book developed gradually over a period of two years, as I learnt of the experiences of some other members of Education Otherwise, the association of parents who educate their children out of school. I contacted my former tutor from Maria Grey Training College, Phyllis Pickard-Bailey, who wrote me a very encouraging letter on her 80th. birthday, which gave me the necessary confidence to embark on this project. A book of this nature would be impossible without the help of the very many parents who have written to me. To all, I would like to say "Thank you." I am especially grateful to those who have found the writing of their experiences to be very traumatic. One parent wrote with troubles so severe as to be beyond the scope of this book. I hope she contacted the NSPCC, as I suggested, and that they were able to help. I have made many friends during the making of this book, both parents of troubled children and those who were, themselves, victims of school phobia in their younger days.

The support of the membership of Education Otherwise has been invaluable. Felix Polkowski and his students deserve special thanks for the typing. Sue Newman's help in gathering information has been invaluable; as has Freda Wynmclean's help in reading and discussing the text and giving valuable advice on many occasions; and Simon and Caroline Grant have allowed me to use their word processor. I am also grateful to the following people for reading through the text and making constructive comments: Simon and Caroline Grant, Sheri Pritchard.

I thank the authors of the two articles from the Education Otherwise newsletter for permission to use the articles. Like the other contributors to this book, they will remain anonymous for the protection of their children. 'The Daily

Express' has given permission for the use of the article 'Truant Tragedy'. Janice Bennett has written the poem.

The staff at Holyhead library have been helpful at all times.

I have had support and been provided with information from the following organisations:-

Education Otherwise, 25 Common Lane, Hemingford Abbots, Cambs., PE18 9AN.

Parents Against Injustice, "Conifers" 2 Pledgdon Green, Henham Bishops Stortford, Herts.

Children's Legal Centre, 20, Compton Terrace, London N1 2UN.

Samaritans – a telephone service for people depressed and in despair. Number to be found in the telephone book.

STOPP – The Society of Teachers Opposed to Physical Punishment, 18, Victoria Park Square, London, E2 9PB.

LET THESE MEMORIES DECAY

by Janice Jazzamine Lorraine Bennett

Sunday crept in fast
The ugly morning looks sombre to me.
The skies seemed frightened to me
My fear begins to occur
And I sit alone, falling to the floor.
Blindly fumbling around the room
Dusting, dusty corners where tears have been shed.
Just have to get myself together.
Tomorrow rides in fast and fear is unmasked.

Time was used unwisely
The day was wasted with worry
Now I rest my tired, worried head on the soft pillow.
Two-thirty, still awake, head spinning with thoughts,
Nibbling at my fingernails,
Pacing up and down in dreams,
Picture of the building,
Voices of the noise.

Perspiration trickles down my forehead,
My stomach aches in pain, my head in shame,
Keep saying I must sleep, but I can't bear to be fooled.

Like a trap, as soon as I sleep
I'll see it in my head, then wake to the dread.
My last tear has spoken, my eyes begin to fall,
Exhausted by all the terror
Hope tomorrow never comes.

Monday morning, the sun shines through my window
    pane,
I find there were no fairy tale dreams
I only wept.

Family are buzzing, going off to work now.
Pull yourself together, oh I've got a headache now,
Oh no! I think I'm going to be sick.
Sat staring into water wondering how to overcome it.
Have some toast and marmalade and a cup of tea.
I am crying and my mum says, "Don't look at me."
Play some Dave and think of Ziggy and maybe one day...

Start to walk, passing familiar faces, but not one do I
    recognize.
Could I turn and run and go back another day?
I can see it looming, its got me in it's clutches,
I am wearing its colours.
Looking around me, they are so very happy, all the others.
Picturing the day ahead in my mind,
Fearing all the faces and words unkind.
Home is getting further away.
I see it disappear as me head begins to sway.

There it is. I'm now here.
Collapse in the corner shaking in fear.
A friendly voice speaks as I go weak at the knees.
"What's the matter, Janice?"
"Nothing's the matter with me," with a big brave smile.
As a bucket of tears drown my laugh.
All the voices turn to thousands of faces,
All the faces turn to taunting voices.

Shaking with-in a fear, possession riot inside
I cannot breathe, I gasp for breath,
I am being strangled, I touch my neck,
My face shatters like a glass mirror.
Seven more years bad luck.
In my glass case I stutter, "Yes Missss"

I drop my books and grovel on the floor
As legs trample over me as though I was the court fool.
Stand up close to the wall
Close my eyes to keep my conscious blank,
But I see a million eyes.
Wish I had a sledgehammer to crack it into pieces.
I want to burn this house of horrors,
This nightmare in the day.
I'll go home, I must get away.
"Janice, Janice! Hurry up, you will be late."
"Just coming," I say with a smile,
And turn to be sick.

Open this door, give me the key to this prisoner door,
A prison without a key. That's the worst of all.
I run into the open air
Staggering for my life.
If I stay, I'll surely die.
What makes me feel this way?
Its always been the same.
I am going home and never coming here again.

And so to this day, I cannot return to the school,
Just to look at it makes me crack.
How could anyone know how I wanted to go,
And would give up everything just to retire.
So I'll remain in a funny kind of sane
And try to forget those memories
Of every day, let them all decay.
I bury them all in a steel coffin.

TROUBLED CHILDREN: A FRESH LOOK AT SCHOOL PHOBIA

INTRODUCTION

My first encounter with school phobia was in a small village school where I was a young teacher. It was a school with only 50 pupils and a very happy atmosphere, so neither 'the headmistress nor myself had any idea what caused the little boy in question to be so frightened. He came to school on only one day when I was at the school. He came with a bodyguard of parents and grandparents who delivered a frightened looking boy to school. Although the children had been told to be as kind as possible to him, and they obviously tried hard to be nice to him all day, it was the only day he came. He was on the register as absent for about one and a half terms, after which he had a tutor who came to his house. He was very humanely treated.

Until I had personal experience of the problem, when my own child became school phobic, I was fully in the belief that all such children were treated in a humane fashion. But not so. I was told to send my suicidal child to school, to ignore the suicide threat, and to allow the EWO ("truancy officer") to drag her to school each day.

I joined Education Otherwise, (an association of parents who teach their children out of school) and discovered that I was not alone. There appeared to be many other families who had had similar experiences, where the education and psychiatric personnel had either disregarded the problem as non-existent, or had meted out harsh treatment to the family, with threats of court cases, care orders and psychiatric hospitals.

One parent whose children were threatened with emergency care proceedings unless they attend psychiatric hospital said, "They treat criminals with more understanding than school phobics".

It is not until a child refuses to go to school that we discover that underneath the veneer of democratic civilisation, our society is like a Police state. I have spoken to a parent who has been handcuffed, and has spent a night in a Police cell. Many, many children have lost their liberty under care proceedings. An institution in which an individual loses his or her liberty is a prison. Why do we euphemistically call such an institution a "home"?

The results of these inhumane treatments are very frightening. Between 60% and 70% of the children forced back to school by any of these methods, grow up to be adults prone to mental illness. This is, however, considered to be success because, in the intervening time, the children have attended school. I can think of no other area where such deplorable results would be considered success.

My aims in writing this book are: to expose injustice; to encourage parents whose children are suffering in this way to educate them out of school; to suggest to the social, psychiatric and educational welfare services that they rethink the policies in respect of these children; and to indicate areas of change within the educational system, so that fewer children will become frightened of school.

All the personal stories I tell are, unfortunately, true.

My policy has been to use fictitious names throughout, as many of those corresponding with me have asked for complete anonymity. This policy has been waived only in the case of the newspaper article.

CHAPTER ONE

The Nature of the Problem

There are two groups of children who attend school infrequently. These are the truants and the school phobics. According to the theories developed by child psychiatrists, these are two very different groups of children, but, in my opinion, this is not so.

In both these groups there is a preponderance of children who are shy and timid. The groups differ in their reaction towards suffering. The one set of children runs away, and the other set of children internalise their sufferings. Internalisation of suffering has grave results. i.e. suicidal behaviour, mental breakdown and psychosomatic illness.

Children displaying these reactions are not treated kindly by the "caring" professions.

The psychiatrists' theory is that school phobia is caused by "separation anxiety". i.e. the child is afraid of parting from mother. Mother is, similarly, afraid of parting from her child. "Separation anxiety" is in turn a result of "pathological dysfunction of the family". This theory was formulated in 1956 and, as a result, during the last 30 years, children who are desperately unhappy and frightened at school, and who internalise their sufferings, have been treated in a way which is an infringement of basic human rights.

Convinced that this theory is correct, psychiatrists have subjected these children to all sorts of indignities. They will be threatened with removal from their parents. (Threats of court cases, care orders, residential schools and psychiatric hospitals). Under threat about 50% of the children will return to school where they will be unlikely to do well. They may be manhandled into the education welfare officer's car (polite term for "truancy officer") and driven to school each morning.

If these methods fail, more drastic measures will be taken. The child may be drugged; may be taken to court and subsequently taken into care; sent to a residential school; or he or she may spend several months in a psychiatric unit, anything, in fact, to remove the child from the "pathological" environment of the family.

In his book 'Truancy and school absenteeism', Ken Reid states that a large majority of the truant children in his study said that it was bullying which made them frightened of school. School phobic children are also frightened of bullying and the other negative aspects of school: ridicule, intimidation, corporal punishment and the stress of very large numbers of people. However, in the latter case, the psychiatrists believe neither the children nor their parents.

It is only recently (1985) that, in his study of truants, Ken Reid actually asked for the opinions of the children. In all previous studies of truancy, the total blame for the situation was placed on the family background, and the opinions of the children themselves were ignored, discounted and disbelieved.

Phobias

A phobia is defined as an excessive, irrational and uncontrollable fear of perfectly normal situations or objects.

There are many different phobias. Very often a precipitating event can be found during the early life of a person, but in many cases the precipitating factor is not known, lost in the depths of the subconscious.

Phobias, according to Eysenck's classification, ('Fact and Fiction in Psychology') are one of the expressions of what he calls 'disorders of the first kind'. Such a disorder 'consists of

18

conditioned emotional responses of an unadaptive kind, probably acquired as a consequence of some traumatic event, or perhaps, in many cases, as a consequence of several sub-traumatic happenings.'

One 55 year old person told me that she was incapacitated by her claustrophobia. She has recently been to hospital and the terror which she felt when taken in the lift was practically uncontrollable, and she had difficulty in preventing herself from screaming out loud. The trouble started when she was five. Her teacher shut her in a cupboard as a punishment. No doubt the teacher achieved the results she wished for. The very active little five year old became a timid, quiet girl who did what she was told. However, the effects of that punishment can be felt by the recipient 50 years later.

One mother did not understand her daughter's sudden fear of the dark. It was not until 20 years later that the girl told her mother that she had been locked in a cupboard by a teacher at the age of five. Children are generally too frightened to tell their parents when an incident of this nature occurs, so, many times, as in this case, the parent only discovers what has been happening many years later, if at all.

Although one would like to believe that this sort of thing only happened in "the bad old days", I have been told by a child that he saw the punishment occur as recently as 1980.

One of my children had the misfortune to be ill when four of her teeth were developing. The result was that they grew without any enamel. When the dentist saw her decaying set of baby premolars (she was only three at the time), he decided to fill them. He assured me that if she had some valium medicine, which he prescribed, she would forget the experience. She did not. Her teeth needed further treatment each year. Each time she was given the valium medicine. She has grown up with a phobia about dentists.

One person, at the age of 11, was riding on a big dipper at

the fairground when the machinery broke down. She spent quite a long time at the top, unable to get down. This experience has left her with a phobic fear of heights.

A phobia appears to other people to be an irrational fear. There are many aspects of schooling were a fear reaction is not at all irrational response, such as bullying, intimidation, ridicule etc.

The definition of a phobia is: an excessive and irrational fear of a perfectly normal situation. A school is hardly a normal or natural situation. It is a highly unnatural collection of individuals of the same age in an institution, unlike society and the family where people of all ages talk and do things together. It is considered by all the powers that be, that such an institution is the most efficient means of imparting knowledge.

For these reasons "school phobia" is a bad term. "School refusal" might be better but "refusal" carries connotations of "being naughty" to many people; also "refusal" is a term which is unlikely to be associated with such extremes as nervous breakdown, suicidal depression or very acute anxiety. A better term would be "acute school induced anxiety". However, I will continue to use the term "school phobia" and "school refusal" as these are the terms used by the psychiatrists and other officials.

Official estimates of the incidence of the school phobia vary widely. Joy Melville, in her book 'Phobias', puts the number as 1 in 700 of the school population. Hersov and Berg in 'Out of school' put the number much higher, at 1% of the school population. Dr Richard Wolfson, writing in the Times Education Supplement (1985) puts the percentage as high as 1.7% to 2%. Ken Reid (1985) puts the figure as low as 0.01%

Assuming that the number lies somewhere between 1% and 2% this would mean that in a school population of around 9 million (England and Wales 1985) there would be between 90,000 and 180,000 children affected. (Ken Reid's much smaller figure would give about 1,000 school phobics).

CHAPTER TWO

"Separation Anxiety" and other Theories

"School phobia" is a term which was invented by psychiatrists in 1941. The term "separation anxiety" was invented in 1956. This is now considered by psychiatrists to be the underlying cause of all cases of school phobia. According to this theory, which is now commonly held by school educational psychologists, social workers and GP's in addition to psychiatrists, the child becomes afraid of parting from mother; mother is similarly afraid of parting from the child. The negative aspects of school: bullying, intimidation, ridicule, etc. are ignored as being totally irrelevant .

In view of the fact that there is a dramatic increase in the incidence of school phobia, at ages 12 and 13, at the age of transfer to enormous, depersonalised schools, this is a ridiculous theory. Why should a child of this age suddenly become afraid of parting from mother? Even more surprising, why should mother suddenly become afraid of parting from her child? The literature on the subject is full of allusions to "overprotective mother", "manipulative child and colluding mother", "pathological dysfunction of the family", etc. (Hersov and Berg, et al., 'Out of School').

In view of the above theory, any means, however inhumane or however costly, may be used to remove children from the "pathological" environment of their homes, and get them back to school.

"Separation anxiety" is caused, so the theory says, by "pathological dysfunction of the family". However, I maintain that anxiety on the part of the parent in the face of a child's deep distress is a perfectly normal reaction and that be "pathological" if the parent were not anxious.

    time the psychiatrist is called in, there have already

     ny arguments about school attendance, and the family will be in the grip of a complex of negative emotions: anxiety, fear (that a suicide threat might actually be carried out), shame, bewilderment and guilt. It is this complex of negative emotions that the psychiatrist sees and labels "separation anxiety".

My own child who became school phobic, far from being afraid of leaving mum, was considering running away from home.

There may, indeed, be such a thing as separation anxiety but it would only affect very young children and would probably be caused by enforced separation from the mother at a very early age, perhaps by hospitalization. Fortunately, the dangers of separating very young children from their parents at this traumatic time are now understood and it is normal for mothers to accompany their child to hospital.

The disproportionate number of children who have been born prematurely and who later become suicidal (Kosky 1983) would point to the dangers of separating the newborn baby from his or her mother which is of necessity caused by placing these little ones in incubators. I am pleased to see that at least one London hospital (Hammersmith) is now discouraging the use of incubators in favour of having the tiny babies on their mother's bodies to draw heat from them. 'Doctors have discovered that premature babies thrive better for being kept with their mothers than if they are in incubators. By being in touch with their babies, mothers are able to tell directly that they are alive, rather than have to check via a monitor. Doctors at Hammersmith Hospital found their babies are less restless when nursed in close contact with mother's skin. "We don't know why the baby is more contented next to the human body, it could be the mother's heartbeat." mused a (male) doctor.' ---- Sunday Times, December 1984.

In the case of true separation anxiety, to forcibly part a child from his or her parents is surely the most doubtful form of treatment.

"Separation anxiety" as the underlying cause of school phobia is regarded by psychiatrists as being a proven fact whereas it is in reality an unverified and probably incorrect assumption.

Eysenck, professor of psychology at London University, has drawn attention to the fact that the Freudian ideas underlying psychoanalysis, and psychoanalysis itself, are highly suspect. 'In question are not only the actual diagnoses used, and their definition, but also the ability of the psychiatrists to apply the labels in any consistent fashion. Several experimental studies have shown that when different psychiatrists in one and the same hospital are asked to give independent diagnoses of a set of neurotic patients, agreement among them is not much in excess of what would occur on a chance basis.'

I would make precisely the same accusations against the originators of the idea that "separation anxiety" is the underlying cause of school phobia. I feel tempted to take Eysenck's words about psychoanalysis, and apply them to this case. 'In this field we are dealing with theories, hypotheses, hunches, surmises, opinions, beliefs – often held with great tenacity and proclaimed with considerable vigour.'

School phobic children should never be educated at home. This is the categorical statement in 'Out of School' (Hersov and Berg et al) based on no research whatever; based on a theory which is quite probably incorrect.

They go on to describe methods of returning these children to school. 50% will return under threats alone: threats of removing them from their homes and families, threats of care orders, residential schools or psychiatric hospitals. The first method of "treatment", where threats fail, is for the child to be dragged to school by the E.W.O.

Where this also fails the next approach may be to drug the child, take him or her into care, into a residential school or into a psychiatric unit. The treatment which will be used, will be chosen according to the particular approach of the psychiatrist concerned, rather than taking individual differences of the children into consideration.

One example given in the book is of a 14 year old boy and his parents who were invited to meet the psychiatrist in school. Once there, the boy, presumably kicking and screaming, was held down by two teachers while his parents were escorted off the premises. They had been tricked into attending what they had thought was an interview. In any other environment, such behaviour would constitute assault.

In another case, the authors tell of interviewing a child and his parents. As usual, they were looking for reasons for the child's behaviour in the family relationships. They found that the father was a compulsive stamp collector and the mother was obsessively houseproud. On the grounds that this constituted "pathological dysfunction of the family", the poor child was taken into a psychiatric unit for seven months.

The impression one gets from reading this book is that children are being treated like experimental rats, worse than experimental rats. If rats, in such an experimental situation, squealed as much as the children forced back to school have screamed, the experiment would be swiftly terminated.

According to the authors of the book, all the methods of returning the children to school are equally successful, i.e. the majority of the children (about 60%) return to school afterwards – the fact that they no longer perform well is irrelevant. So also is the fact that between 60% and 70% of the children later develop into adults prone to mental illness. This is not success. It is DISASTER.

Later on, in chapter nine 'The story of John', is a detailed account of the harsh, unfeeling treatment meted out to one child, and the circumstances leading to his subsequent nervous breakdown. Such a sequence of events is probably repeated in the lives of thousands of children.

In Ian Berg's study of 100 school phobic children who had been treated in a psychiatric hospital: after only three years, 33% showed signs of severe psychiatric disorder, and a further 33% showed signs of mild neurotic trouble. This is 66% disaster, and it is quite inexcusable that the author calls this success and that others (psychiatrists, psychologists, social workers, doctors and educationalists) believe him. In any other circumstances, such results would be deemed to be failure.

We are talking here, not of inanimate objects, but of human beings and their lives; of avoidable mental illness. Apart from the suffering inflicted by mental illness on the patient and his or her family, there is also the considerable cost to the country as a whole, of unemployable adults, of sickness benefit and of hospital places.

In this country, until quite recently, corporal punishment has been legal in all schools. Viewed from the children's point of view, this is a case of children being bullied by adults. Is this what we want to teach our children? That in our society, it is acceptable for the strong to bully the weak? It seems that our young teenage gangs have learnt the lesson only too well. So too, have the parents of those children who suffer from non-accidental injury at the hands of their parents. There is the occasional shock to the nation, when a child is beaten to death by his or her parents.

A widely read book in the Soviet Union on the upbringing of children (by Pechernikova, and quoted by U.Bronfenbrenner) devotes seven pages to corporal punishment and the damage it can do to young children. It is, of course, forbidden in Soviet Schools.

When we witness destruction in our inner cities, wholesale rebellion by large numbers of adolescents, and an increase in the crime rate leading directly from this, is it not time to say to ourselves "where have these people spent most of their time?". To which the answer is "in school" or "truanting from school". We should then look at the educational system, at the institutions where they are condemned to spend eleven years of their life, to find out what aspects within the system are contributory factors in the social breakdown.

It is not good enough to overhaul the examination system. This may result in more children leaving school with academic qualifications but it will have no effect on the breakdown of our society which we are witnessing today.

I was listening to a phone-in radio programme in which parents were invited to ask questions of a psychiatrist on the subject of adolescents. One mother asked about her teenage son who had been violent towards herself. The psychiatrist explained that two year olds go through a stage of rebelling against their parents, and having tantrums in which they hit their parents; that this child had not completed the process when he was two, and was therefore behaving like a two year old in his mid-teens.

This was no help to the mother, and it is also a very dangerous theory, incorporating, as it does, rebellion as being a perfectly normal phase of development.

It is true that many two year olds are rebellious, but by no means all of them. Two year olds have inquisitive and exploring minds, and are active little people. Selma Greenberg in her book 'Right from the start', puts down the terribleness of two year olds to the fact that these active, inquisitive little people are so often confined in the barren environment of the nuclear family; alone with mother for so much of the day, mother who often busies herself with housework and has little time for the child; confined in a house or flat where there is little chance of interacting with other adults and often without sufficiently interesting occupations. It is no wonder that many of them rebel.

Theories of Western developmental psychologists have

not taken into account any but their own cultures. There are other cultures in which rebellion has no part in development, and also the antisocial or anti-adult peer group has no place. Frank Musgrove, in 'Youth and the Social Order' describes African cultures in which the passage from childhood to adulthood is not marked by a rebellious phase. Urie Bronfenbrenner describes the educational system in Russia which leads to the development of the teenage peer group fully integrated into the society as a whole, and who support and maintain adult standards.

Developmental psychologists would do well to study societies different from our own, and modify their theories accordingly. As long as rebellion and aggressive behaviour is considered normal, rates of crime and delinquency in this country will continue to rise.

The first stage in the development of such a theory observes that many two year olds are rebellious. From this derives the corollary that it is normal for two year olds to rebel. This leads on, imperceptibly, to the next stage, that if a two year old does not rebel, he or she is abnormal and his or her teenage rebellion will be worse, as a result.

The theories describing adolescence follow a similar pattern. Many teenagers in our culture gather together in aggressive groups, therefore it is normal for adolescents to gang together and to bully. From this it is only one more step to say that any child who passes through adolescence without rebelling against his parents, without belonging to a teenage gang, is abnormal.

Many, many parents have written to me with the same story. Parents have explained to the psychiatrists or psychologists that their child is bullied and that this is the reason for the school refusal. The official has then replied that it is quite normal for adolescent boys to group together into an aggressive gang and to bully those weaker than themselves. "It is your boy who is abnormal", they say, "Timid and solitary, he is asking to be bullied. He needs psychiatric treatment."

One family had been educating their boy out of school for over a year after he had a nervous breakdown. He was progressing very well. He had recovered from the nervous breakdown and was being educated by means of a correspondence course. The school had refused to de-register him during this time, and was presumably illegally claiming the £22.00 a week that it costs to educate a child in the state system. (This figure from a 'Sunday Times' article 1985). This also meant that he had been marked absent from school for one year, and the psychiatrist was informed again. The parents were then told that there would be a case conference about the child. They attended, uninvited, and found that it was held behind locked doors. They were later handed a piece of paper with the decision of the conference: that he should enter a psychiatric unit "Because he is not developing normally. He is too happy. At this age he should be rebelling".

Maybe there is a connection between the acceptance of these theories, which incorporate rebellion as being a normal part of development, and with the rise in violent crime and delinquency, inner-city riots, etc. Instead of saying "Where are we going wrong in the upbringing of our children?" the Government increases the police force.

CHAPTER THREE

Educational Methods in other Societies

A.   Russia

School phobia is not a problem in Russia, according to 'Out of School' Hersov and Berg et al.

If this is indeed the case, it would appear to be very important to study the Russian method of education and see how it differs from our own. Urie Bronfenbrenner in his book 'Two Worlds of Childhood' compares the method of schooling in Russia with that in the U.S.A. It is indeed very different.

There is no corporal punishment in Russian schools. Each class is divided into groups. For example, in a class of 30 children, there might be three groups with ten children in each group, with an even distribution of boys and girls, dull and intelligent. There is a system of rewards, not of an individual pupil but for a group. There is little chance that an individual child will be ridiculed by his/her peers and called a duffer or a dunce. Instead, children in the same group will help each other in order that the group as a whole will do well with their work.

There is not the segregation by age that exists in most schools in Britain and the USA. Each class will be given the responsibility of a class of children three or four years younger than themselves. For example, a ten year old class will be given the responsibility of a seven year old class. The ten year old children will be expected to escort the younger ones to school, play with them in the playground, and help them with their schoolwork. The way in which these duties have been performed enters into the assessment of the school report carrying, it seems, equal weight to academic achievement.

The ten year old group is, similarly, linked with the 13 year old class which is, in turn, linked to a group of adults, perhaps in a factory.

The active promotion of social education results in teenagers who behave in quite a different way from the adolescents who gang together in aggressive, anti-adult groups in this country.

The author of this book tells of walking through the streets of Moscow with his young children. A group of teenage boys came round the corner, picked up the little two year old child, passed him from one to another with happiness and joy, playing with the little child. This is not the behaviour we, in this country, associate with gangs of teenage boys.

The peer group in the USSR acts to support behaviour consistent with the values of adult society, it also induces its members to take the responsibility for the development of such values to others.

Urie Bronfenbrenner discovered that it is reasonably safe for women and girls to be out alone at night in Moscow and other Russian cities.

Although he may have been shown schools of which the Russians were especially proud, the results of the educational system seem to make the streets of Moscow safer.

In Britain and the USA, by contrast, the "socialisation" process is unsupervised by the adults, and is age-segregated. It takes place in the playground where bullying, ridicule, etc. are rife. The results of this policy can be seen in the rise in crime and delinquency, the explosive increase in the use of drugs, and the growth of the cult of the teenage peer group, divorced both from young children and from the adult world.

To improve the educational system, we must look, not at the curriculum so much as at the social education which is practically non-exsistant in our schools. We must look to other cultures and see how it is that their upbringing of children differs from our own.

It is laughable that those of us who educate our children out of school are accused of depriving our children of opportunities for socialisation.

B.   Denmark

In schools in Denmark, no corporal punishment is allowed. The school entry age is seven. Danish parents are encouraged to educate their children, not for the first five years, but for the first seven years. When they enter school at the age of seven, those children will have a confidence and poise that is unknown among school entrants in this country. They will be ready for formal learning, which many of our school entrants are not.

At the age of 11, after only four years in school, Danish children have reached an equivalent standard to that of 11 year olds in this country after six years of schooling.

In Denmark, if parents are dissatisfied with the child's schooling or would prefer a different approach, they may form a "small school". A "small school" may be set up by a group of parents, provided they have at least 12 children. At the end of a year's functioning, government inspectors will inspect the "small school" and, if it is found satisfactory, the school will be able to receive an 85% government grant for subsequent years.

'Official attitudes to the "small schools are essentially supportive. They are regarded as a modern expression of Denmark's tradition of intellectual freedom; and are regarded as important sources of pedagogical innovation and as healthy competition for the dominant state education sector.' (Advisory Centre for Education).

Like all other countries, Denmark has a school entry age higher than that in Britain. It is only in this country that we

31

condemn active little five year olds to long hours of sitting still. We should raise the school entry age to six or seven, replacing the first years of infant school with optional kindergarten/playgroup, where the emphasis is on creative activities and play, and where the ratio of adult to children is about 1:8.

As long ago as 1967, the Plowden report on Primary schools recommended that the school entry age should be raised.

As can be seen by comparison with the Danish experience, this would result in no lowering of standards. In fact the literacy rate would probably increase as it is easier for the majority of children to learn to read after the age of six and a half, and fewer children would become discouraged by too early a start.

In the mid 1980's there is much talk about cuts in the educational budget and lowering of educational standards. This is one cut which would have no effect on standards.

When I taught the infant age group, I was disturbed by the fact that some children, five years olds, cried every day for a fortnight when they first started school. How much better it would have been for them if they had had another year to mature before being forced to go to school.

In a study by the Commission for Racial Equality (1985) into differences between children of different racial origin, it was found, among other things, that black children in the infant school cry more than white children because, so the researcher said, they are more neurotic than their white contemporaries. Is it neurotic for a five year old to cry when parted from his or her mother and made to sit still with a crowd of people?. This is not neurotic. Perhaps we have trained all the children who do sit still and quietly in such a situation to behave in a neurotic and abnormal way, candidates for tranquillizers in adult life.

The Danish government gives an 85% grant to any group of parents and teachers who wish to form an alternative school with a minimum of twelve pupils, and provided that they can show the inspectorate that the education provided is adequate. There is no comparable provision in this country.

I fail to see why such a system could not operate in this country. If children were given the option of attending "small schools", there would probably be fewer cases of both truancy and school phobia. Both of these increase dramatically, shortly after transfer to large comprehensives, probably indicating that the large numbers of children in our enormous comprehensive schools are extremely stressful for some children.

C.   China

Selma Greenberg, in her book 'Right from the start', talks about child-rearing in China. From an early age Chinese children are taught vigorous physical exercises.

'Chinese children cared for in group settings spend a large part of their day in doing regular, structured, increasingly difficult exercises, games and dancing. This I saw as the Chinese way of preventing disorder's and promoting good development.

'When I visited China I, like other visitors, was astonished by the children's prowess in acrobatics, gymnastics and dance, abilities already evident by the age of three. These abilities were based on a regular exercise programme built gradually, and starting only a short while after the child began to walk. The Chinese child rearers never confused this activity with recess and free play which the children also enjoy. As a result, their very young children can sit and stand absolutely still. They had a life which balances vigorous activity with quiet time in a well-ordered pattern'

Each of these methods of educating and rearing children

33

has lessons we could learn in this country, and incorporate into our own educational system.

The differences stem, perhaps, from a different philosophy or perspective in the way people view children. Selma Greenberg, on her visit to China found that the Chinese never expect a child to be naughty. They understand that all behaviour, even naughty behaviour, is learned.

CHAPTER FOUR

Stress, Depression and Anorexia Nervosa

A.   Stress

If you are enjoying a quiet walk in the country and suddenly find yourself in the same field as a fierce bull, fear lends speed to your feet. You find that is possible, under the influence of subconscious bodily changes in response to fear, to run faster than you have ever run before. After leaping over the gate to safety your body gradually regains its normal state. Breathing rate and heart rate slow down, and blood pressure reverts to normal.

The extra strength and energy needed for the crisis reaction result from body changes caused by adrenalin being poured into the bloodstream as a result of a fear-provoking stimulus. It prepares the body for flight or to fight.

To run away from a fierce bull, or to turn and fight an enemy are both responses to this hormone.

The effects of adrenalin on the body are widespread. Heart rate increases, blood pressure rises, often to very high levels, and may remain high for some time, blood vessels throughout the body are affected. Those in the voluntary muscles open up so that more blood can flow through them. Those in the abdomen and skin contract so that less blood flows through them. Sweating increases, saliva dries up, secretion of gastric juices increase and the gastro-intestinal tract is markedly affected and more active; bronchi expand, allowing more air to be taken in by the lungs, energy reserves in the liver and muscles are mobilised, making glucose available for immediate energy requirements.

Stress arises when adrenalin is released into the blood stream at a time when flight and fight responses are inappropriate.

People respond differently to the same situation. A situation which is a challenge to one person, to another can be mildly stressful, and to a third can reach the point of intolerable stress. A school which to one child is a challenge, can become an intolerably stressful situation for another child.

Even within one family, there may be one child who finds school a challenge, enjoying both academic and social aspects, another child who finds school very stressful, but becomes an academic success while withdrawing from social contact with his or her peers. There may be a third child who finds school intolerably stressful and becomes school phobic.

While there are some children who find school stressful and become academic successes, at the same time withdrawing from social contact with their peers, there are others for whom social activities and sport are more important, and they fail academically.

Schools vary too, of course. There are some very good schools run on friendly and democratic lines, and with a minimum of the aggression – fear balance, and where there is virtually no bullying. In these schools the stress factors are very low. There are other schools, sadly, where this is not the case, and where both staff and pupils can find life very stressful. If a member of staff becomes ill with stress, he or she may have a nervous breakdown or even leave the school without incurring the wrath of the authorities. Not so a child. A child showing severe stress symptoms is victimised, as is his or her family.

'40% of headteachers in Doncaster have applied for early retirement because of stress leading to illness. Heart attacks, ulcers and nervous breakdown are cited' – Daily Telegraph May 1985.

'In Australia a senior psychologist said that it was

36

common for teachers under stress to develop a phobic reaction and become terrified of school' – Times Educational Supplement, May 1986.

The effects of adrenalin on the body are widespread. The effects of stress can also be widespread, affecting very many different parts of the body and causing a variety of psychosomatic disorders.

A large majority of school phobic children complain of tummy upsets every morning before school, and are unable to eat any breakfast. Some of the children will go on to develop frequent vomiting or diarrhoea, and a very small percentage will progress to the state of anorexia nervosa (The incidence of anorexia is increasing. The number of cases in Sweden doubled over a period of 30 years.)

Headaches are commonly an indication of stress, both migraine and muscular tension headaches. Migraine can incapacitate a person for the duration of the attack, and a tension headache can leave a person exhausted and debilitated at the end of a day.

Asthma attacks can be precipitated by stress, and may be more frequent and more severe under these conditions.

It has recently been found that some schoolboys in the U.S.A already have a thickening of the arteries which is a precursor of heart disease. Diet has been blamed for this – too much animal fat. However similar changes can take place in the arteries as a result of the effects of prolonged high levels of adrenalin. I suggest that it is possible that these changes could be due to the stress of school on some unfortunate, vulnerable and highly sensitive children.

Severe stress can precipitate a nervous breakdown. This occurs when mental conflicts become intolerable. It may be provoked by family circumstances or by the school, or by a combination of the two. Psychiatrists, however, with their propensity for blaming the home, especially the mother, for all such troubles, will investigate only the strains and stress of the family, ignoring completely the effects of the school.

One child, recovering from a nervous breakdown, was persuaded by her step-mother to tell the psychiatrist that it was the school that had caused her the problems. She was hesitant to do this as the psychiatrist talked to her only about interpersonal relations, within the family and with her friends. (And especially about communications, or lack of it, with the other sex.) She at length plucked up courage to mention the fact that school made her terrified. The psychiatrist's response was "Rubbish. There is no such thing as a phobia of school. Don't ever talk to me about it again". Is this the caring, understanding profession?

There are various subconscious methods a person may have of coping with stress. The most useful and positive reaction is adaptation, where the person learns to live with and use a certain amount of stress.

The other subconscious methods of dealing with stress all have very negative effects and can cause problems in schools, possibly lying beneath almost all cases of "underachievement". They are denial, rationalization, projection, displacement, withdrawal and daydreaming, and a hostile and aggressive reaction.

Perhaps the withdrawn daydreamer is reacting to stress. Perhaps the hostile, aggressive child is also reacting to stress. These are two very different reactions to a stressful situation: the one contributing to underachieving pupils and, if the stressful conflict is severe, predisposing towards nervous breakdown; the second, the hostile reaction, contributing towards the breakdown of society.

The displacement reaction towards stress is the factor which comes into play in anorexia nervosa, as worries about school are transformed and become worries about food.

Other more conscious attempts to cope with stress are by the use of smoking, alcohol and drugs.

In a Sunday Times article on smoking by children (1985), all the children, in reply to the journalist's question, said that they had taken to smoking in order to overcome stress. At a time when it is becoming realised that smoking is injurious to health, and many adults are giving up the habit, more and more youngsters are taking up a habit which may shorten their lives.

Drug abuse is far more likely in a person who started smoking at a very young age. Does this mean that drug addiction among young people, one of the gravest social problems of the 1980's, and a growing problem, is a response to stress, largely the stress of school?

Why do we condemn children to 11 years of schooling, if it can be such a stressful situation for a large minority? How can we change the educational system so that it becomes a less stressful environment? Is the fact that more and more adults become dependent on minor tranquillizers linked to the degree of stress in their lives as youngsters? (At any one time, two million people in the U.K. are taking minor tranquillizers for anxiety).

Judging by the results of schooling in Denmark, the school entry age could be raised to seven with no falling in standards, whatever. This, besides being in the interests of the children, would have the incidental effect of cutting the education budget. In Belgium, the ratio of staff to pupils is 1:8. It is not surprising that educational standards in that country should be the highest in Europe. Working in such small groups is probably also far less stressful for both children and teachers.

The educational system should be modified and become far more flexible, with grants available for the formation of "small schools"; and where parents are actively encouraged to educate a child at home following a school crisis. Although I am thinking chiefly of school phobia, there is also the question of daydreaming children (daydreaming can be a response to stress). These children, also, might be able to concentrate more easily at home.

Truants, also, would probably benefit from home education at least for a time.

Some children, after being home-educated for one year,

decide to return to school. They should be free to make their own decisions about their education.

B.   Depression

Feelings of depression are common enough; feelings of gloom and dispondency in response to life's ups and downs and which generally pass in a day or two. Abnormal depressive states do not pass. The feeling of depression which brings in its train a host of negative emotions, coupled with physical and mental fatigue and which continues for months, or perhaps years, is abnormal.

Women suffer from depressed states about twice as frequently as men. This is significant because a depressed mother can cause depression in a child. Postnatal depression which is caused by hormone disturbance, and can be overcome by hormone therapy, is particularly significant as it affects the child's first view of life and his or her relationship with mother. The formation of the mother-child bond can be adversely affected by the mother's postnatal depression. The non-formation of the mother-child bond can lead to disturbances in behaviour patterns in infancy and childhood: to a baby who cries a great deal and later grows into a child with severe behaviour problems.

Maternal depression can strike at any time, because the life of many women is a depressing condition. We cope with broken nights, crying babies and demanding children and at the same time unpaid drudgery and monotonous housework. Kathy Nairne and Gerrilyn Smith in their book 'Dealing with depression' call this a recipe for disaster.

In his book 'Bonds of Depression' Gordon Parker speaks of depressed adults who seek help from psychiatrists to overcome their depression and are who encouraged to talk about troubles from their infancy and childhood. The psychiatrist can then infer whether there has been faulty attachment to the mother or mother figure. In many cases, they see that a faulty mother-child bond underlies the tendency towards depression.

A faulty mother-child bond can be caused by "under-bonding", where the mother-child bond has failed to develop properly and the child has grown up unable to relate to a mother figure; or it can be caused by "overbonding". This is, in Parker's view, caused by an over-protective parent who does not allow the child freedom to break away from family ties.

This is a plausible theory, but it leads to parents being blamed for circumstances which are often beyond their control.

In maternity hospitals, it used to be the case, until 1977, that babies were separated from their mothers and only brought to them at four hourly intervals. Although this suits the sleep-pattern of many infants, others who did not fit into the routine were left to cry for long periods of time. If this treatment has continued for a few days, it can result in a behaviour pattern setting in with long periods of crying, and it is impossible for the optimal mother-child bond to be formed. The crying pattern of the baby can lead imperceptibly to the development of behaviour patterns which can disrupt the childhood development and can leave a caring mother extremely frustrated; and sad, because she recognises that the bond she had hoped for between herself and her child is non-existent.

In his paper 'Childhood Suicide Behaviour', Robert Kosky noticed that children who become suicidal are disproportionately represented from the group of children who suffer from birth trauma or were premature. Similarly, Ken Reid mentions that there are a disproportionate number of children who were premature babies amongst the truant group. As it is usual for premature babies to be removed from their mothers and placed in incubators, it is probable that both of these groups of children have made unsatisfactory bonds with their mothers. They then grow up as troubled children.

Then we, the mothers, are blamed.

Faulty mother-child bonding can also be caused by what G. Parker calls "overbonding". This results from an overprotective mother, or other parent figure, suppressing the growing desire of the child for freedom. Although this does undoubtedly happen in some cases, a great many mothers are being labelled "overprotective" when in fact they are not, so.

If a child becomes either truant or school phobic, the blame is immediately placed on the parents, especially the mother. A poor home background is often assumed to be the sole reason why a child becomes truant i.e. the parents are blamed. An "overprotective" mother is taken to be responsible for the troubles of a school phobic child, or the child is labelled "manipulative" and the parent "colluding"

Owing to the very nature of this book, I have heard chiefly from families where the members have been poorly treated by psychiatrists. There are undoubtedly psychiatrists who have been far more sympathetic than some of those I have mentioned in this book. I have, in fact, one letter from a 19 year old girl who is full of praise for the treatment she received in hospital after her nervous breakdown at the age of 15.

The schools' psychiatric teams tend to blame mothers, but blame has no part in psychiatry. It is no part of psychiatry to build up people's guilt. There is to much emphasis on the mother as the cause of all the problems, rather than social factors such as school and peer group.

In order to remove children from this so-called "pathological" family setting all sorts of methods are devised, expensive and inhumane, to get the child to return to school, or to remove him or her temporarily or permanently from the the family.

It is obvious to those of us who are caught in this

situation that the psychiatrists are unable to distinguish between an overprotective parent and a parent who is genuinely concerned about a troubled child. At any time when a psychiatrist is called in, he will see a family under stress. The parents are worried about their child. To see in this natural anxiety only "separation anxiety" is a gross impertinence. To make threats of care orders, court cases, etc. is only to compound the anxiety. To follow the threats up by actual removal of the child is a disaster for the family.

There are parents who have written to me, where it is obvious that the child has been troubled since birth, with prolonged crying in infancy and severe behaviour problems in early childhood. This is obviously the result of what Gordon Parker calls "underbonding". If this leads on to school phobia, the mother is accused of being "overprotective" i.e. "overbonding". The psychiatrists are even unable to distinguish between "underbonding" and "overbonding", but convinced they are right in their diagnosis, they will recommend, perhaps, the removal of the child from his or her parents into care, into a residential school or psychiatric hospital. In any of these situations children may be drugged as a form of social control.

> 'The Children's Legal Centre claims that young girls in care have been forcibly injected with Largactil and Valium, and others put in solitary confinement for up to 36 hours in Lambeth.'
> (Guardian, Nov 1983)

As a result of these inhumane treatments, about 60% or 70% of the children will grow up with psychiatric or neurotic problems. Some of them will have psychiatric troubles so severe that they will be unemployable.

One parent writes to me of her days at school:-

"When I was in my teens, my day's timetable was as follows:- After getting up at 7 a.m., I left the house at 7.45, to walk the mile to the bus stop and catch the bus shortly after 8 o'clock, to the school where I felt lost in the crowd and under great stress except during biology lessons which I enjoyed. For several years I had no friend in this milling crowd of 1,200 people. (It was one of the first comprehensive schools). I suffered from a recurring nightmare at this time – of being a very small child trapped in a crowd of very much larger people.

"After school was over, we waited in a crowded classroom for the bus to arrive a quarter of an hour later. I arrived home at 5 o'clock. After a meal, I had one hour of relaxation before two hours of homework, from 7-9 o'clock, by which time I had to think of bed because of the early start I had in the morning.

"This was a day full of stress, with one hour of relaxation. Is this how we wish to train our children, under conditions of so much stress? During the seven years at the secondary school, I completed O and A level exams successfully, but never learnt how to socialise. I was afraid of that sea of people, and have spent my adult life trying to overcome the fear of people which I learnt in school.

I also spent one and a half hours every day on a bus. In the seven years that I spent at this school, I would have spent 2,100 hours sitting on a bus, if I had been to school every day, 2,100 hours of wasted time. However, I did not go to school every day as I was frequently ill. Every year I had a bad attack of 'flu and I also suffered from frequent severe ear infection. I am convinced that I was susceptible to so many infections because I was living under such stress.

"On one Saturday, I started to cry uncontrollably at the thought of the homework I had to do in the weekend. My mother, who knew that one of my schoolmates had just become ill with a nervous breakdown, sensibly put me to bed. I had breakfast in bed, was given some light reading and then given lunch in bed. After lunch, I got up and was forbidden to do any homework that weekend. Fortunately, the weather was fine and I divided my time between gardening and walking in the country, with a little light reading from time to time.

"During the 13 years I had been at school, the lesson which had been drummed into us most successfully, was to sit quietly. This did not stand me in very good stead when I went for interviews. I did manage to get a university place, despite the fact that I spoke mostly in monosyllables at the interview.

"After being trained in an atmosphere of stress, I have been prone to long periods of chronic depression in my adult life. Sometimes I have been prescribed antidepressants for three months at a time, and felt as though I was rattling with tablets, as I struggled to lead a normal life through the feelings of blackness and despair".

One mother writes:-

"After my child became suicidal at the age of twelve and a half we educated her out of school. As I am a trained teacher, I was able to embark on this despite the authorities disapproval. My child is a very intelligent and sensitive child, and we embarked on study towards ordinary level GCE exams, with the idea of continuing with art study at the local polytechnic.

"As the time for exams drew nearer, she started to

suffer from headaches and feelings of nausea. I was dismayed that it looked possible that my highly intelligent child was finding the prospect of exams, and working for them, to be too stressful. She looked as though she was one of those people that could not cope with exams.

"When she saw the doctor, she had by now become very weepy. He diagnosed depression and advised her only to work in short spurts of half an hour, with a break in between. He also told her that a great many children, in school, suffer from depression in the exam year.

"When she told me in this latter fact, I became very angry. Why don't the GP's rise up with one voice and say that the examination year is too stressful for a great number of children?

"If it is known that exams can cause chronic depression in large numbers of children, and sometimes mental breakdown, why do we continue with the system? The examination system is much too stressful; to expect children to study for and sit possibly eight or more subjects at one time. Is it beyond the wit of man (or woman) to invent a different system?"

'The Samaritans are receiving more calls than ever from school children worried and depressed about exams' – Times Educational Supplement Dec. 1984.

'A 17 year old American shot his mother dead because she was angry about his poor school report.' Daily Telegraph, May 1983.

C.   Anorexia Nervosa

Anorexia nervosa is a severe form of psychosomatic illness. It is also a potential killer, though much less common than the other potential killer – suicide attempts.

The first letter I received on the subject of school phobia was from a mother, two of whose children had become severely troubled at school. One had had a nervous breakdown and the other anorexia nervosa. It was at that moment that I realised that anorexia, suicidal depression and nervous breakdown could be manifestations of the same problem.

Two percent of patients with anorexia nervosa actually commit suicide, and quite a large percentage make suicide attempts, sometimes even before any loss of weight has occurred. Dally and Gomez, the authors of the book 'Anorexia nervosa' underestimate these suicide attempts by calling them suicide "gestures" or "token" overdose and, in spite of these facts, anorexia nervosa is not considered by these authors to be associated with depression.

According to these authors, anorexia nervosa is caused by a fear of growing up, and a distorted fear of sex, and is only aggravated by the academic pressures of schooling. I would suggest, however, that the pressure of schooling and academic achievement can be in many cases the underlying cause for the eating disorder.

All patients with anorexia nervosa come from social classes 1 and 2. About 10 times more girls develop this disorder than boys. Almost all of them are intelligent, attractive adolescents who are very concerned with their academic achievements, and who come from families where academic achievement is important. The proportion of children who develop this disorder is five times higher in boarding schools than in day schools. This points to the fact that it is definitely linked to schooling and that boarding

47

schools put too much stress on these pupils, either because they are total institutions, giving pupils no respite from their fellow-pupils, or because they have been selected by their parents as schools with a reputation of high academic standards and this puts too much academic pressure on the child.

Many children who are school phobic complain of stomach pains, lose their appetite, or vomit in the mornings. It is only a short step from this to anorexia nervosa. Suicidal depression, with loss of appetite, can also merge imperceptibly into anorexia.

In the study by Dally and Gomez, many of the patients with anorexia nervosa had had feeding problems when they were younger, or had mothers who at one time had had to diet severely in order to lose weight. In both these instances the family's attention had been focussed on food. This probably predisposed these children to focus their anxieties upon food, so that a nervous breakdown, when it took place, took this form. Anxiety over school work is displaced to become an anxiety over food.

This points to the inadvisability of forcing young children to eat when they do not want to. Long-term food problems may be set in train, and also the possibility of the later development of anorexia.

In 'Catherine,' by Maureen Dunbar, the mother tells of her daughter who died of anorexia at the age of 22. She had been force-fed by an aggressive father in her early childhood. Later, at boarding school, she had stopped eating. Towards the end of her life she said "The only way I could make myself ill was to stop eating, and the only way for me to be allowed home was for me to become ill." If the child had known it was possible to be educated at home, tragedy might have been averted. Anorexia nervosa can take control of a person's body, as the starvation affects the hormone from the hypothalmus, and the person's metabolism is severely altered.

It amazes me that psychiatrists should think it significant that people with anorexia nervosa are uninterested in sex, and that therefore it is obvious to psychiatrists that a distorted view of sex is the underlying trouble. On the contrary, I would think it extremely odd if someone whose body was in a severe state of starvation should be interested in people of the other sex in a sexual way.

Dally and Gomez imply that the fact that many of the girls they had interviewed had forgotten the date of their last menstruation was significant, pointing to the probability that these patients were afraid of sex. Why should this be so? On the contrary, girls who are obsessed with the dates of menstruation would be, to my mind, abnormal.

The theory that girls subconsciously "know" that starvation will prevent their menstruation and that they starve themselves with the intention of preventing this, thus proving to the psychiatrists that they are indeed afraid of sex and of growing up, is another idea which is extremely doubtful.

The child I mentioned at the beginning of this section was subsequently educated at home by her mother, despite pressure from authority figures that she should enter a psychiatric unit. ("Would I ever have seen her again if that had happened?" said her mother). When the stress of school had been removed, she gradually regained her appetite and recovered from her illness. At the end of three years of home education she was looking forward to continuing her studies at the local polytechnic.

CHAPTER FIVE

Methods of forcing children back to school or into other institutions

As a counterbalance to the unhappy tales I have received, here are some happy stories. I have only received three letters telling of how the problem was overcome within the school. I will include them all:-

A. One parent told me that she was at her wits' end when nothing would entice her child through the school gates. She says, "We beat the school phobia problem with the help of the headmistress."
The headmistress invited both mother and child into her office, made them very comfortable and talked about the whole week's timetable, encouraging the child to talk about anything in any lesson which she found difficult. The headmistress then spoke to each of the child's teachers in turn. All the teachers in that particular school were so understanding that the problem resolved itself easily.

B. "I phoned the headmistress who had a reputation for being strict and unyielding. However, she listened sympathetically and suggested I take Brenda into the office next morning. This I did, and after a long chat with both of us she concluded that Brenda liked her form teacher (the history teacher) so suggested that Brenda stay with her throughout the day. This entailed her sitting through history lessons at all levels; but she stayed.

"I had to take her into the front hall (normally out of bounds to the girls) and obviously the head had done her job and, subtly, a teacher would appear and say, 'Hello Brenda, will you help me with this?' or words to that effect. I could then leave her reasonably happy.

"One morning a teacher said 'Would you help me feed the rabbits?' This was the turning point. She took over looking after the rabbits, and if she didn't go to school, they didn't get fed or cleaned. Within a month they had her back in normal school routine and she never looked back! The school has my sincere thanks!"

C. One girl, who went to a very small comprehensive school on one of Britain's offshore islands, became school phobic. The school was small enough to treat all the pupils as individuals and to adapt itself to suit this particular child.

In some LEA's there are special classes for school phobic children. These contain a group of perhaps 10 children, a group small enough for these children to feel happy and able to learn. Children in such a situation are humanely treated and can develop their potential.

Some LEA's provide a home tutor. This is excellent while it lasts but all too often, after a certain length of time, the child is told to return to school, often with the use of drugs.

The other ways in which children may be treated are far from humane.

1.   Threats

The first method is the use of threat. Under threat (of court cases, care order, psychiatric units and residential schools) 50% of the children will return to school. Should threats have any place in psychiatry? The children who return to school under threat are unlikely to perform well academically. ('Out of school' L. Hersov and I.Berg , et al.) I find this hardly surprising.

2.   Education Welfare Officer

The second line of attack is for the EWO to drag the child, often kicking and screaming, to school, the EWO probably uttering threats at the same time. "You must come to school with me like a good girl/boy. You don't want to be one of those naughty children who is taken into care"

In one case the EWO came into the house and said, "How many of us are there? You, me and his big brother. Good, I'll take one leg, you take the other and his big brother can take his arms. That way we'll get him into the car".

In another case, the EWO dragged the child downstairs. The child held on to the bannisters which broke. If the bannisters had been stronger, the child might have dislocated his arm. This is legalized assault.

If the above methods fail, any of the following may be used.

3.   Child Guidance Clinic

At the child guidance clinic there is a multi-disciplinary team consisting of child psychiatrist, educational psychologist, social worker, with possibly a child psychotherapist and a remedial teacher. Each member of the team carries the theories of "separation anxiety" in his or her mind, and will see any anxiety within the family as a manifestation of this.

The school phobia is seen as a displaced manifestation of conflict between the child and parent or of pathological overdependence. This results in a complete breakdown of communication between the psychiatric team and the family, as every complaint about the school, be it bullying children or intimidation by a teacher, is interpreted as a reflection of a conflict in the home.

a). **Psychotherapy** may be used to investigate and "treat" the conflicts between child and mother.

b). A system of **desensitisation** may be used. By this method progressive moves back to school are made, together with learning a system of relaxation exercises. The first few sessions will consist of talking about the school situation and the expected return. This is followed be taking the child to school in the car, sitting in the car and looking at the school building, and waiting for the feelings of panic to die down. The next session will consist of taking the child to the school when there is no one there, and either staying in the playground or entering the school building when it is empty, again waiting for the panic to subside. The final session under this system will be for the child to return to school.

c). **Family Therapy** This is designed to investigate relationships within the family, on the grounds that it is these which are the root cause of the problem. Although the attempt to unravel some family discord can be useful, in helping the family to understand and remedy conflict, this is no use at all in resolving difficulties in school, which have been caused by the school and where the family interactions are positive.

If however, there is stress within the family it is bound to compound any stress at school.

d). **Behaviour modification** The fallacy of this approach rests not on the behaviour therapy as such, but on the assumption that a fear reaction in response to school is an abnormal reaction. This by no means necessarily the case. Faced with bullying, intimidation, extortion etc. fear is a perfectly healthy reaction.

The Children's Legal Centre, in its magazine 'Childright', 1985, has recently drawn attention to the fact that behaviour modification techniques are, in the opinion of the workers at the centre, an infringement of human rights. Behaviour modification is a system of rewards and punishments designed to result in modification of behaviour patterns resulting in this case in a return to school.

David Weikart has recently completed a 20 year follow up study of the effects of nursery schooling for pre-school children. The effects of three different types of nursery school were studied, and there was an adequate control group.

The following is quoted from the Times Educational Supplement (April, 1986):

'Three carefully matched groups of disadvantaged children whose IQ scores classified them as slow learners at risk of school failure were randomly assigned to three different pre-school programmes.

'One group followed the traditional nursery school approach, emphasising social and emotional growth and learning through children's interests and free play.

'The second followed High/Scope's own

curriculum, which shares the belief that children learn through their own first hand experience. The curriculum provides teachers with a clear framework designed to promote the acquisition of fundamental concepts and supports systematically the development of children's abilities to initiate their own learning.

'The third followed a behaviourist approach, directly teaching disadvantaged children basic academic skills such as counting and letter recognition, in a programme of teacher directed activities each with specific objectives.

'The children were followed up at ages five, six, seven, ten and 15. Up to ten there was no significant difference between the three programmes. All three boosted the mean IQ of the children from 78.3 at age three to an astonishing 105 after one pre-school year.

The startling differences between the programmes came at age 15 on social, not academic, measures. The group from the behaviourist pre-school class had committed twice as many violent and delinquent acts as the teenagers from the other groups.

'They had gone in for twice as much drug abuse, and five times more damage to property. Their behaviour was very similar to the control group.

'Dr David Weikart, High/Scope president and director of the research emphasises that because of the small numbers (68) these results cannot be seen as conclusive. They are, however, a very strong signal.

Although perhaps not directly relevant to behaviour modification, this casts doubts on the application of behaviourist techniques to classroom settings and to very young children, and indicates that it can have hazardous and unforseen consequences at least in certain circumstances.

A detailed account of the High/Scope project may be found in 'Young Children in Action' by Hohmann, Banet and Weikart. Although this describes work with pre-school children, many of the ideas are relevant to education at all ages.

Dr Weikart's research casts grave doubts on the behaviourist approach.

In a book by Nigel Blagg, 'School Phobia and its Treatment' he states that he has had great success by his method, the "confrontation" approach. By use of his scheme, which may include the use of force, he has the children "happily" back to school within two and half weeks. He describes a boy who clung to the kitchen table leg, and who was dragged to school, his fingers being prised from the leg of the table. Within the two and half weeks, the boy was attending school in a docile manner.

This, to my mind, is not necessarily success, since my criterion of success is the development of the child into a balanced adult.

A case was brought to my attention which is very similar to Nigel Blagg's case. A girl, a nine year old, was forcibly carried into school by three adults. Like the child mentioned by Nigel Blagg, the girl subsequently went to school in a docile manner. However, she became very withdrawn, and by the time she reached school leaving age, had developed anorexia nervosa and had lost her will to live. Her mother wrote me a very distraught letter.

It seems quite possible to me that the child Nigel Blagg talks about will similarly suffer from some form of mental trouble.

4.   Drugs

Children may be drugged. In a society where drug addiction among young people is a severe and increasing social problem, this is an extraordinary method of treatment. The drug normally used is imipramine (Tofranil) which is a powerful tricyclic antidepressant with some very severe side effects: tremor, similar to Parkinson's disease, constipation, dizziness, blurred vision, palpitations, urine retention, excessive sweating, weakness, fatigue and headache. Too high a dose can cause epileptic fits, overdose causes fever, high blood pressure, seizures and coma. Even with smaller doses, chronic disturbance in heart rhythm can occur. It is, in fact, necessary for children on the drug to have an electrocardiograph which is, of course, a test for heart disturbance.

One mother tells me that the severity of the side effects affected her son so badly that he screamed with terror, they were so horrible and frightening.

It is not known how imipramine acts, but it is believed to effect the chemical messengers at the synapses between neurones in the nervous system.

It would be far better for children to be educated at home rather than to be given such a dangerous drug.

Other drugs used for school phobic children when forcing them back to school are: phenelzine, chlordiazepoxide, phenobarbitone, amytriptyline, diphenhydramine, amphetamines and diazepan (valium). They can produce many unpleasant side effects; three of them are addictive, and some of them can produce quite severe withdrawal symptoms.

Sometimes a tranquillizer may be used simultaneously with a powerful antidepressant such as imipramine.

In their book 'The Myth of the hyperactive child' Diane Divoky and Peter Schrag tell of almost a million children in the USA in 1975 who were drugged, usually with Ritalin (an amphetamine type drug) as a means of social control. If a child was labelled "hyperactive", Ritalin was prescribed by physicians and psychiatrists, under pressure of advertising by the drugs companies who had invested four million dollars in the development of the drug. Ritalin calms an otherwise active child and makes him or her sit quietly in class. The pressure of the advertising campaign of the drugs companies was aimed chiefly at the middle class parent, especially the mother who, concerned about her child's education, would hurry the child off to the doctor. The drug has not been used to any great extent on black children, as the parents tend to be very wary of drugs administered by white professionals.

When the rules of direct advertising of drugs were changed, the drugs companies changed their tactics. Instead of advertising the drug, they now advertised the ailment, eg, "If your child is hyperactive, take him to the doctor ."

The results of this policy have had grave effects. The side effects of Ritalin are: loss of appetite, serious weight loss, insomnia, depression, headaches, stomach-aches, bedwetting, irritability and dizziness. It can also, in rare cases, cause paranoia, both visual and tactile; or psychotic behaviour. Long term effects include liver damage. Some children's growth has been stunted to such an extent that they have become "bone thin and zombie like"; others have become drug dependent adults. In a society where the explosive rise of drug abuse is a grave social problem, this is an incredible way to treat children.

True hyperkinesis (hyperactivity) is rare, affecting 1 in 2000 people, and may be found to be caused by a certain component in food, possibly a food additive, which has a toxic effect on some individual's metabolism, causing behaviour disturbances. In the U.S.A. in 1975, however, "hyperactivity" came to mean any behaviour which offended the teacher and could be equated with "won't sit still" or "learning disabled", and reached epidemic proportions. Using threats of expelling or suspending their children from school, parents were intimidated into seeking medical help. "In the guise of creating tests for diseases, the diagnosticians created diseases for the tests."

Some children can be shown by medical tests to have very slight brain damage which impairs learning. On this basis, other children who had difficulty in learning might be labelled as "learning disabled" or as having "minimal brain dysfunction". "Labelling a child as learning disabled qualifies for a grant. Children are labelled, money is claimed as children are removed from mainstream class and put into special classes. Any child who annoys the teacher can be got rid of like this, and the money claimed. The label usually becomes part of the child's personal record."

Besides Ritalin, (methylphenidate hydrochloride), Dexedrine (dextroamphetamine) and Cylert (magnesium pemoline) and a few other drugs are used. Most of the children who are recipients of these drugs are between 6 and 13 years old, but some children are as young as 2 when the drug is prescribed. The drug may be given over a period of several years, into adolescence and beyond.

The idea that people's behaviour should be controlled by drugs is a very dangerous one, and not at all what one would expect in a democratic and so called "free" country. In some ways a "safe" drug, with no side effects, would be even more dangerous. Large scale administration of such a drug could produce a nation of puppets, manipulated by those in power.

In the 1970's there was an effort to detect "predelinquents" in order to treat them and thus prevent delinquency. A controlled experiment in preventative intervention was carried out 'Treatment involved Ritalin, psychotherapy, behaviour modification, the placement of children in special classes, etc. The results of this intervention were completely negative. More of the "treated" group became delinquent than in the control group.'

The authors give an example of a boy who received this intensive treatment because he lacked what the teacher thought should be the reading skills of a seven year old. After four years of "treatment", his verbal IQ had dropped from 127 to 97; and his overall IQ dropped from 137 to 117. 'They had reduced the child from being an unusually bright boy to being an ordinary problem'.

Other methods of social control are also mentioned. Some schools have experimented with placing a child who is easily distracted by his or her surroundings into a cardboard cubicle to do their work, when parents have refused to consent to the use of drugs. There are even children, seven years old, who have had brain surgery to try and "cure" this imaginary disease.

5.   Court Cases

If threats of court cases are insufficient to make a child return to school, the family may be taken to court. In some areas, it is the policy to adjourn the case, in the hope that the child will return to school in the intervening time between hearings. A child may be taken to court several times before he or she is eventually taken into care, or similar. Parents have told me of distorted or even untrue evidence in psychiatrist's reports, which may be used to persuade the magistrates to make a care order.

Adjournments of Court Cases

The following article first appeared in the Education Otherwise newsletter.

Alice's mother writes:-

> "To encourage children to attend school, our LEA has been experimenting with the procedure of repeated adjournments in the Juvenile Court.

Each time the child appears and it may be at intervals of a week, a fortnight, or more, depending on progress, the child's attendance is reviewed. If attendance has not improved, an interim care order is made as an 'encouragement' to attend school. If this does not work, a full care order is made. The chairman of the magistrates tells the child in no uncertain way of the consequences of poor school attendance: 'Next time bring a bag with your night things. You'll be going a way for a bit.'

"Alice was nine or ten years old when she first started feeling ill. It went on for months before I pinpointed it to Friday's games day. One teacher at Middle School was a bully. After having a word with the headmaster who said I was not the first to complain about the teacher, she stopped picking on Alice but became sarcastic and sneering.

"After about a year of this, Alice became worse, and taking her to school became a nightmare. She would feel sick from getting out of bed, and feel sick all the way to school. Sometimes I would take her to school, asking her teacher to keep an eye on her. I was always at the doctor's surgery, and when Alice started with pains in her legs and stiffness, I really began to worry.

"She was sent to hospital to see a specialist. She had blood and other tests but thankfully they could find nothing wrong. Alice continued feeling ill: she was acquiring new ailments all the time. She would go to bed at night and shout down 'I can't breathe!' She would be gasping for breath. I would sit on her bed and talk to her, or read a story. This would help for a while, and then it got worse.

"I took her to the doctor who said it was asthma.

In time I found it easier to go to bed with her. She also moved into my bedroom as by now she was very frightened. We would spend most of the night awake. Sometimes we sat in the garden at two a.m. to help her breathe. I could not send her to school after a night like that, but I always took her to see the doctor. He wanted to examine her for asthma so that she could be given a spray. But he could not, at the time, as she alway's seemed full of cold.

"The EWO became a regular visitor to our home, and twice made Alice get out of bed to be taken to school. Quite often she would be sent home as she would faint in class or be sick. I have had to carry her home many a time if she had fainted on the way to school. No one could convince me that she was not seriously ill. The EWO asked my permission to check with the doctor that we did attend the surgery, and at the time I did not realise what this meant. He left a card with the doctor to be put in her medical folder to be filled in every time she attended. It was about six months before I found this out, and as a result I became on such bad terms with the doctor we were asked to leave the practise, even though he had been our doctor for over 40 years.

"One night Alice was so ill with asthma, we sat up all night with the washer hose fixed to a boiling kettle to help her breathe. She was so bad that her dad stayed up with us, even though he had to be up at four a.m. for work. Later that morning I telephoned the doctor who sounded concerned and said she would come right away. As she came into the room, she took the EWO's card out of the medical folder and her whole attitude changed towards us.

"She examined Alice quickly and told us if we were worried to get a bottle of mixture from the chemist; no prescription was given. I asked: 'Could it be night asthma?'. She said she did not know anything about it, and left rather abruptly. Next day Alice was no better, so I made an appointment to see another doctor at the surgery. Before I went in to see him, I took the EWO's card out of my folder and put it in my pocket as, with it, I did not think we would get fair treatment. (After it had been discovered that patients were given their own medical folders to hold, and that Alice's mother had abstracted the EWO's card, arrangements were changed at the surgery, so patients were no longer handed their folders to hold, and such a thing could never happen again).

"The doctor said she had bronchitis made worse by asthma, and could not understand why the other doctor had not noticed this. I told him he did not have the card, and showed it to him, saying it was not to be put back in the folder. But before we left, the doctor tried to help us. He gave her an asthma spray, but said he thought she had school phobia and referred her to a Child Psychiatric Unit.

"We had already made our first appearance in the juvenile court, but during the six months that Alice was at the unit, we did not have to go to court. The time at the unit was useless, as it was used only to try and induce her her into thinking that school was the best place to be and that all her illnesses were in her mind.

"One day, travelling to the unit by bus, a lorry ran into the bus while it stood at the traffic lights. Some of the passengers were taken to hospital by ambulance. The others were put on anotner bus to continue their journey. Alice was in a state of shock when she arrived at the unit, and told the sister why she was late. She received no sympathy, and was told to go into class and get on with her work.

"The first I knew of it was when she came home at four p.m. with a stiff neck and a croaky voice. I took her to the hospital. She had a back injury and whiplash. She had to wear a collar for weeks.

"I telephoned the sister next day and asked her why Alice had been treated this way. She said: 'We don't take a lot of notice of these kids as they often come in late with excuses.' She telephoned the bus station to confirm my story, and apologised.

"After six months she was sent back to her own school, and back to court. Her attitude to school had not changed. In fact, it was made worse by being away for so long. She did not find it easy to fit back in. She was asked by the other children where she had been. Twice she was ill at school: once she was left to sit in the corridor all afternoon, the other time the head teacher bought her home.

"By now my nerves were in a very bad state. I dreaded getting her up on a school morning to be told she felt ill. My heart used to be in my stomach as I forced her to go to school; and because of this, I punished myself by not eating all day. At work I feared the telephone ringing in case it was for me to collect Alice from school. We could not go out any more in case she was ill. It was awful.

"In September 1984 Alice was to move to High School, and she had chosen an all girl's school. We hoped things might change, but it was just the same, and now it was costing me £20 a week in taxi fares to get her to school. In her condition, travelling by bus was difficult.

"Halfway through the term I read an article in a newspaper about educating children at home. I had heard about it a few years ago, but the EWO said that I had no chance. I got in touch with the author of the article who came to see us, but when he heard that we had a court order on us he said we not find it too easy. We joined Education Otherwise and were put in touch with other families with the same problems. We found this a great comfort as we had felt so alone.

"By now Alice had turned against me. We were going through a bad time at home. She thought I did not know what she was going through. She became bitter towards me: coming home from school glaring at me and staying in her bedroom all evening. If I spoke to her she snapped back.

"Alice passed out one day in the dinner queue. I was sent for and I began to wonder how much more either of us could take. And she was so withdrawn, I was frightened for her and what she might think of doing.

"The chairman of the magistrates caused many problems. I had earlier been to see the solicitor who refused to take our case because of this man. So we had to face him alone and believe me, he was as bad as I had heard. It seems he put together the system in our town and other magistrates dare not go against him. He is reluctant to lift a court order from a child brought before him for truancy, although it was said that Alice was not classed as a truant. He terrifies children into going to school with all sorts of threats. It was never a very pleasant experience going to court, but it was made worse by this man.

"At the time of one appearance in court Alice was having trouble with her periods, a touchy subject for a girl so young. He shouted some abuse across the court room, embarrassing her. She had visited the doctor earlier that day. The EWO said in court that he had telephoned the doctor, but the doctor said he not seen her. The magistrate went wild and although Alice had good school attendance, he said his usual piece: 'Next time, bring your night clothes, as you will not walk out of this court with your mother.' He would have had her put away for Christmas.

"When I arrived home, I telephoned the doctor to find out why he had said Alice had not been to see him. We had not told the new doctor about the court cases, so he did not realize how serious it was and I explained what had happened. The EWO had telephoned the leading doctor of the group practise, who told him he had not seen Alice that day and could not find her medical notes. They were still on the desk of the doctor who had seen her. This mistake could have put Alice in care.

"The next time we went to court, was just before Christmas. It was the time my eldest daughter, Ann, lost the child she was carrying. The night before we went to court, Alice stayed the night at Ann's house looking after her two year old son, while her husband and I rushed Ann into hospital. I did not send Alice to school that morning and, as we were in court that afternoon, I hoped it would go unnoticed. They knew she had not been to school. We had not been to the doctor for a cover note.

"The magistrate asked if she had been to the doctor, and when she said no, but had not slept that night, he said: 'Right you're away this time, my girl, and they will make sure you get sleep where you're going, as they give you sleeping tablets.' At that I had had enough; for the first time I let him know what kind of temper I have. I screamed and shouted at him, and told him why she had not been at school that morning. He was shocked for a moment, then said he was sorry for what had happened and would let Alice off this time. I suppose he thought we should have been grateful to him, but I told him we did not need his pity.

"I would listen to the other children in the waiting room saying what they thought of him and what they would like to do to him. With this hate in their souls, it made me wonder where they got rid of their aggression; maybe at the home of some poor old woman.

"Through EO we appointed a solicitor who had no experience of this sort of case, but was prepared to give it a try. I suppose he saw it as a sort of challenge. It was worthwhile for us, as now we were getting some respect in court. Alice was even allowed to sit down, and this magistrate did not shout quite so much. The solicitor asked the magistrate to take the court order off Alice, but he would not.

"In February 1985 we decided to take Alice out of school and gave as an explanation: she cannot be educated in two places at once. It was a month before we went to court again and during this time a senior EWO came to visit us. He saw Alice working and said he knew our intentions were genuine, and would say this in court.

"When the chairman of the magistrates learned that Alice was being educated at home, he was not amused. He wanted her back in school.

"At court we saw a pleasant woman magistrate.

She said it was hard work teaching your own at home, but wished us luck. She could not take the court order off us, as it was the previous magistrates case.

"Another month, another court case and a different magistrate. This was a man, and he wanted Alice back at school. He took some convincing of our case. We were in court a long time that day and her books were sent for to help the magistrate reach his decision.

Happily, our solicitor had really done his homework; the magistrate had to concede, saying that how the next hearing went would depend on an assessment of her work.

"We were visited by an LEA senior adviser. He seemed pleased with what she was doing. So in June 1985 there was nothing else the court could do but take the court order off Alice. At least we had won! We never did see the chairman again, and we have not heard of him since."

During the time Alice had been in the psychiatric unit, she had never once seen a psychiatrist. It was just like school without the holidays, with the occasional group therapy thrown in from time to time. It was her mother who saw the psychiatrist, once a month. "To tell you the truth," her mother says, "all he was interested in was my sex life," in true Fruedian tradition!

6.   Care Orders

Children are often taken into care for non-attendance at school even when parents are willing and able to educate them out of school; in some cases, even, when the children have been educated out of school for some time, using a correspondence course or employing a tutor. Why is it called "care"? It is an institution in which a child loses his or her liberty. An institution in which an adult loses his or her liberty is a prison. Punishments for running away from a children's home are severe, and may result in the child being removed to a more prison-like institution, a secure unit.

Secure units are claustrophobic in design, allowing less area per inmate than the minimum stipulated for modern adult prisons. In a typical modern prison the area per inmate is 69 square metres; in a secure children's unit the area can be as small as 33 square metres. Add to this the lack of adequate recreational and educational facilities which lead to boredom and frustration and which aggravate the children's problems. 'Placement in security may increase a child's resentment against and alienation from institutions in particular and society in general, even if that child's behaviour within the institution is docile and compliant.' ('Development of Secure Units in Child Care' by G.J. Blemental)

Children are routinely locked into their bedrooms at night.

The only outside areas for recreation are very small when compared with modern prison standards. There is often only a small courtyard enclosed by high walls. It is little wonder that, after confinement in such a unit, some of the children pass directly into adult prisons or adult mental hospitals. Most of them spend at least part of their adult life in such institutions.

The inmates of secure units may include children who have committed serious offences, children who have run away from open community homes, and suicide attempters. The latter two sets of children have obviously been extremely unhappy in an institutional setting. How strange that professional "carers" should put their most unhappy children in prison.

The punishment for not attending school when in "care" can be up to 48 hours in solitary confinement ('Childright', 1985). In such circumstances there has been at least one completed suicide in recent years, and very many cases of "self inflicted injury". This is a euphemism for a suicide attempt.

This account was sent to me by a Grandmother:-

"Barry is my grandchild and I have looked after him since he was a very small child.

"One day when he was six he fell off the climbing frame at school at nine o'clock in the morning and broke his leg. The teacher sat him on a chair where he remained for the next two hours. At 11 o'clock the headteacher telephoned me to say that Barry had hurt his leg, and would I take him to the doctor.

"The doctor felt Barry's leg, Barry screamed, 'Don't touch it.' Then the doctor diagnosed a simple sprain, and left.

"Soon after this, I took him to the hospital but, because of all the delays, this was not until 2.30 in the afternoon, five and half hours after his fall.

"As a result of all the delays, his leg took eight months to heal. Naturally, when he returned to school after this accident, he was petrified of school. From then on, getting him to school became a nightmare. My neighbours helped me by taking him in their car, but he used to walk home on many occasions. It was such a struggle, and I felt I was near to a nervous breakdown.

"His attendance became worse over the years, and eventually, at the age of 15, he was taken into care. When he ran away from the children's 'home' because he was so unhappy, he was assaulted and grabbed violently by authority figures, and dragged back to the 'home'.

"After he had been in the 'home' for three months, my boy had become like a cabbage. It was then that I read an article which told me that it is possible to educate children at home.

"I took my boy out of the children's 'home' and employed a tutor, but the treatment he has received over the past few years has left him with emotional scars."

I have heard from someone who was placed in care about 20 years ago, for non-attendance at school. She says," I cannot believe such terrible things still happen to children."

While in the institution, she developed an ulcer and, because there were no facilities for caring for a sick child in the 'home', she was put in a remand centre with petty criminals. While she was there, she was locked in her bedroom each night with nothing but her mattress.

She says, "It is the worst form of child abuse there is."

She now suffers from severe agoraphobia.

7.   Psychiatric hospital

There are various means by which attendance in a psychiatric unit may be enforced. One, apparently innocuous, method is for the psychiatrist to explain to the parents that this is in their child's best interest. Worried parents, anxious to do the best for their child, acquiesce.

Attendance in a psychiatric unit may be enforced by a court case. It may also be enforced by the threat of a Place of Safety Order. A Place of Safety Order gives the local authority powers to remove a child from a battering parent (the police may help them in this). It should be used in no other circumstances. It is therefore a gross misuse of emergency

71

powers to use it in this case. The family is then forced to send the child into the psychiatric unit, otherwise he or she will be taken into care.

One child was taken into a psychiatric unit because his parents had been convinced that it would be in his best interest. He tells of being forcibly held down by two nurses while another member of staff gave him an injection "To calm you down". He also tells of being forced to take drugs mashed up with jam; and of the day when he was given a packet of sweets by his parents when they visited him. These were snatched away by a nurse, after his parents had left, with the words, "You can't have them. You are too naughty". Later he saw his sweets being distributed to other children who were "good". This is behaviour modification in action.

Group therapy will probably be used in a psychiatric unit. I have spoken to an adult who has recently spent time in hospital following a nervous breakdown. She says "Group therapy strips people of human dignity. I have actually seen two people reduced to the most dreadful tears on two separate occasions. It can be very degrading. Only those people who are strong enough to resist are not degraded."

Few people have this moral strength following a nervous breakdown.

The following account describes both group therapy and family therapy:-

> "My mother was advised to take me as an impatient to our local psychiatric hospital. I was 14 at the time so I went to the children's unit which, as far as I was concerned, was as bad as school; but, looking back, it was probably worse, as the set up was so bizarre. Children from around five or six years, with problems ranging from epilepsy and broken homes to slight retardation were jumbled together, played games and had rather riotous discussion groups about their problems. It was all

very bleak and tatty, and some children had evidently been there for years, and I felt I might be, too".

She then passed her 15th birthday and entered the adolescent unit.

"At that time I analysed my fear as being towards institutions, and the black depressions – and they were black – which had engulfed me when trying new schools, engulfed me now, particularly early in the mornings when I would lie awake, terrified of a life which made these demands on me, terrified of the months ahead until my 16th birthday when my life would be my own again.

"The treatment was carried out in group meetings where we were supposed to discuss and share our problems. Again, this was the 'treatment formula' they stuck to, convinced that it was effective. In the three months that I was there, I never saw it helped any of us; most people sat in silence, and on one uncomfortable occasion no said a word all the way through. After the day staff had gone home, however, we, the patients, used to chat quite a lot.

"One horrific feature of the treatment was the 'family group meeting' which even I dreaded, but were frightful for children of divorced parents, etc. A social worker would talk to us and encourage my parents and brother and sister, nine years and four years older than I am, respectively, to contribute. I used to feel very embarrassed and guilty about what I was putting them through. My father never used to comment. He'd never been all that talkative. My mother and my brother used to try and be helpful and compromising, without the least idea why I was as I was, or how they could help – bar the support they gave throughout. My sister was very angry, feeling I should have been pushed off to school, and used to be silently mutinous, so the whole experience was uncomfortable and unproductive.

"The climax came when my mother decided to remove me. I only had to go back, they said, for one meeting with the charge nurse and a couple of others. During the meeting they insisted that I should stay and ended up sending my mother home without me, which, after all my assumptions that I had finished with that place, was very traumatic.... I was told that my mother felt I was too dreadful to have at home and wanted me to stay. However, when my mother discovered what they'd told me she'd said – which she hadn't at all – that was the end for her too, and I was taken away for good."

It is not surprising that 12% of child suicides occur in local authority care and other institutional settings if this is the way the inmates are treated. (0.6% of the child population is in Local Authority care. 1985 figures) The rate of child suicide is thus 20 times as great in institutional settings as it is in the child population as a whole.

In their book, 'The Heart Of The Race: Black Women's Lives In Britain' Bryan, Dadzie and Scafe publish an account given by a young black girl of her treatment in a psychiatric hospital. She talks of being put in a straight-jacket and being left in a room with no windows, and with nothing but a mattress, and a bucket for use as a toilet. This punishment was meted out for the crime of crying.

In this institution, all the girls were given tranquillizers in the daytime and sleeping pills at night. This particular girl refused to be drugged, but not openly, or she would have been forced. She pretended to swallow the tablets but actually hid them. At the time, she had no intention of making a suicidal act but eventually she became extremely depressed by the whole environment, and by the fact that she had no idea how to get out of the institution. Her relatives had been forbidden to contact her by telephone.

Finally, in a feeling of desperation, she took all the tablets and lay down to die. She was found, and salt water was poured into her by a stomach tube, and she was made to vomit. She was then locked in the punishment room, with the mattress and the bucket, for 24 hours. When she beat on the door to asked to be released, she was forcibly injected with a sedative, and told to remain there for a full 24 hours.

On the following day, she managed to "sneak out and phone my grandmother" who had been trying to telephone her, but had been told she was not able to speak to her granddaughter. By the time her grandmother arrived, the girl was again in the punishment room. "They told her she couldn't see me but my grandmother didn't take any notice of them. I was banging on the door and I heard her ask me if I wanted to come home and I said 'Yes'. They were arguing with her, and saying that she can't take me home because she wasn't my mother, but she took me home, though, there's no way they were going to stop her once she realised what was going on. I was 15 when this happened.

The authors comment, 'It is little wonder that those of us who enter such institutions relatively sane frequently end up by displaying precisely those symptoms which our incareration was designed to cure.......

'It is experiences like these which have led to a disproportionate number of young black women to leave school and enter a lifetime in and out of institutions...... ensuring that the State's short term solution is likely to become our long term problem.'

At the end of the time in the psychiatric unit, it may be decided that, instead of returning to their normal school, the child should instead attend a residential school. I am not sure whether the parents have any say in the decision.

8. Residential Schools

These are either schools for backward children or for maladjusted children, and for those who have been in trouble with the police. Under the influence of such a peer group, the child's behaviour may rapidly deteriorate. One parent wrote to me that her child had started glue-sniffing and developed delinquent tendencies in such a setting. It is likely that other children might become even more withdrawn in the face of the violence and delinquency of their companions.

Edmund

Edmund's primary school days passed relatively uneventfully and peacefully but, at the age of 11, on changing to the comprehensive school, he developed severe behavioural problems.

He was expelled from more than one school, started bedwetting and then glue-sniffing.

Edmund and his mother saw both the child psychiatrist and the educational psychologist. Mother found them "incredibly naive and their replies stereotyped." At the time, she thought their advice was good, but she realised later "what a total failure their system was".

Edmund was then sent to a "school" for "children with special needs" i.e a "school" for "maladjusted". At the "school" (his mother always uses inverted commas when she speaks of it) he mixed with boys who had criminal records. No real schoolwork was done here; the boys were treated like babies and responded by developing criminal tendencies.

As a direct result of attending this "school" Edmund developed criminal behaviour and was finally taken to court, facing a charge of Taking and Driving Away. The headmaster produced a report saying that Edmund had influenced the other boys (but it was the other boys who had criminal records, not Edmund). The headmaster's report also stated that Edmund would not talk about his parents to the headmaster, and recommended that he should be taken into care (why should the fact that that he does not want to discuss his family life with the headmaster be held against him? asks his mother indignantly)

Mother kept Edmund at home for a few months after this. His behaviour improved, and he stopped sniffing glue.

After this, he went to a private school for a while. This was fairly successful; but he had arguments with authority figures. He has now been removed from school and will be educated at home.

His mother says: "I would like to see the system changed, as, at present, there seems to be 100% failure rate; but the state slavishly follows the philosophies of dead geniuses, which bear no relation to life in the 1980s'

Another parent writes:-

"The child psychiatrist's first conclusion was that as I sat with my daughter throughout the home visit (he sat next to my husband – which was normally 'my' seat) my husband was neglected! I couldn't believe what I was hearing and had no faith in any of his other theories. He later suggested my daughter went to a 'school' in a nearby town. I should have known better. He thought she might be bored in school and need 'stretching'. However, it turned out to be a school for all kinds of social misfits. The first questions were: 'Can you write your name?' and 'Can you read this?' (a simple childs book). Well, she ran

77

away and was picked up by their transport – an old ambulance – and deprived of her clothes, made to wear a nightdress all day – this, for a 12 year old in a mixed group – was not only degrading, but asking for trouble, I thought.

"Naturally her phone calls home were distressing, and my instinct was to bring her home! But what next?

"I had to sign that I was taking her home against medical advice!!!

"I then approached our local convent school and they were extremely helpful. My daughter cried every day for about six weeks, most days, all day. The staff were amazing, every one. When I thanked them for their patience, kindness and understanding, Sister Bridget said 'We are looking after a very sick and unhappy little girl.'

"One teacher walked the grounds with her and sat and ate her sandwiches with my daughter at lunch time, and talked to her.

"Eventually she settled down and reached a reasonable academic level and, most important, was happy.

9. Fines

The following is the form sent out to parents by one LEA when a child fails to attend to school. There is no mention of the option of home education which also contained in Section 36 of the 1944 Education Act.

'WARNING TO PARENTS
'Section 36 of the Education Act, 1944, places a duty on parents of a child of compulsory school age to

cause that child to receive full-time education

'I am directed to inform you that your child_____ has/have been absent from _____ school and I have to urge upon you the absolute necessity of your child_____ in future making regular and punctual attendance, in order to avoid proceedings being taken against you.

'TAKE NOTICE. If your child_____ is/are absent through sickness and proceedings were taken against you it would be necessary for you to prove that your child was absent for that reason. It is, therefore, advisable that you send a medical certificate to the Head Teacher whenever your child is absent because of sickness.

'You do not have to answer this letter and may wish to seek the advice of a solicitor. You are not obliged to say anything or send a written reply unless you wish to do so, but what you might say may be put in writing and given in evidence if the matter comes to court.

'The maximum fine is £400 for the First and Second Offence and on the Third Offence a fine of £400 and /or imprisonment not exceeding one month.'

Since the option of home education is not mentioned, this amounts to intimidation of the parents.

My colleague Sue Newman has had some heartrending phone calls:-

"I will never forget that phone call. It was from a public phone box and the lady was crying. She did not leave her address, so that I was unable to contact her afterwards. Between her tears, she told me, 'There will be a court case this afternoon, and my son will be taken into care.'

"Nor will I forget the call from a distraught father. He told me that his son had spent twelve months in a psychiatric hospital and now he had been placed in care, in a remand home with other adolescents who were waiting to go to Borstal for theft, burglary, etc. This was all because his son was too frightened to go to school. If any proof is needed that the treatment given in a psychiatric hospital is ineffective with cases of school phobia, it would be this case. This child had spent twelve months in a psychiatric unit. At what cost to the taxpayer?

"When he was younger, the boy was bereaved. He lost his mother. Having lost his mother, he was then removed from his father for a whole year, and has now been placed in an institution in which he has lost his liberty.

"The father was so distressed by the turn of events that he moved away from his home and I was unable to contact him again. He was completely shattered. First he had lost his wife, through cancer, and now he had lost his son."

In a period of twelve months, Mrs Newman has had over 100 telephone calls from distraught parents.

How much taxpayers money has been used in all these inhumane enforcements?

CHAPTER SIX

Legal Requirements of the Education Act

The United Nations Universal Declaration of Human Rights, article 26, states:-

1. Everyone has a right to education.
2. Education shall be directed to the full development of the human personality.
3. Parents shall have the prior rights to choose the kind of education that shall be given to their children.

   Section 36 of the 1944 Education Act states that it is the "duty of the parent of every child of compulsory school age to cause him to receive efficient, full-time education suitable to his age, ability and aptitude, either by regular attendance at school or otherwise".

   Section 37(i) "If it appears to the Local Education Authority that the parent of any child of compulsory school age in their area is failing to perform the duty imposed on him by the last foregoing section, it shall be the duty of the authority to serve upon the parent a notice requiring him, within such time as may be specified in the notice, not being less than 14 days from the service thereof, to satisfy the authority that the child is receiving efficient full-time education suitable to his age, ability and aptitude either by regular attendance at school or otherwise.

   Section 39(i) "If any child of compulsory school age who is a registered pupil at a school fails to attend regularly thereat, the parent of the child shall be guilty of an offence against this section."

   Section 76 "so far as it is compatible with the provision of efficient instruction and training and the avoidance of unnecessary public expenditure, children are to be educated in accordance with the wishes of their parents."

From the above, it can be seen that both the 1944 Act and the United Nation Declaration of Human Rights give parents the right of choice in their children's education. The association of parents who teach their children out of school have taken the world "otherwise" from the Education Act and call themselves "Education Otherwise".

It should in theory be relatively easy for parents to make an "otherwise" decision in education. In actual fact there may be many stumbling blocks. The first stumbling block is that we are never told our rights. Every parent of a pre-school child should know that there is the option of home education. In a democratic and free society, we should know, so that we can make an informed decision. Is an autocratic school the best environment to educate a child for democracy?

At any time when there is a school crisis, be it truancy, school phobia or whatever, the parents should again be told their rights. It is quite possible that the parents of all school phobic children would want to educate their children at home. This policy would probably result in far fewer of the children growing up with a proneness to mental illness.

It is possible, also, that a considerable proportion of the truants' parents would like to educate at home. There is a proportion of the truants' parents who are perhaps illiterate. In this case, of course, it would be impossible for the parents to supervise a child's education at home. It would, however, be possible, and probably cheaper in the long run, for a tutor to teach both the child and the parent to read, after which time the parent could supervise the child's education.

Section 76 states that pupils are to be educated in accordance with the wishes of their parents "so far as it is compatible with ...... the avoidance of unnecessary public expenditure." All sorts of expensive and unnecessary means are used to force children, truants and school phobics, back to school when a much cheaper solution would be for the parents to supervise the education of a child at home.

How much public money is unnecessarily spent on EWO's, court cases, care orders, residential schools, psychiatric hospitals, etc?

How much does it cost the nation that over 60% of the school phobic children, after this treatment, become adults prone to psychiatric troubles? How much does it cost our society that quite a large percentage of the truant group grow up with delinquent and criminal tendencies? Perhaps our society would be a less 'sick' society if these two groups and their parents were encouraged to involve themselves in home education.

The UN Declaration of Human Rights states that "Education should be directed to the full development of the human personality". Many children lose too much of their self-confidence at some time during their schooldays. This confidence is of vital importance in the development of a full personality. For these children, education in a family setting might be far more profitable, not only in the academic field, but also in developing the children's social skills. It is a modern fallacy to believe that school is the ideal place for learning social skills.

A school is an artificial environment where the competitive nature of the classroom leads to a few children who feel successes, and the majority who feel themselves to be failures. Even in the best of schools, the competitive nature of the classroom leads to jealousy.

Teachers who call children "slow", "duffers", "dunces" and "lazy" can do untold damage to the self-confidence of such children. It should come as no surprise that the children who truant in the primary school are mainly those who are labelled by their teachers as "lazy". (Hersov and Berg et al). If I was eight, nine or ten years old or younger, I would want to run away from the place where everyone

83

called me "lazy" and made insulting remarks about my ability. Probably many of these children have been expected to understand numbers and reading at too early an age, and have become confused and frightened. If the school entry age were raised, fewer children would become confused in the early stages of formal learning and would be labelled "lazy". These would have a two-fold consequence. Literacy and numeracy should both improve, and there should be fewer truants.

'Truancy rates at Inner London schools are now running at more than 19,000 a day'. Daily Telegraph, March '86.

CHAPTER SEVEN

Reasons for School Phobia.

According to the commonly held view of psychiatrists, all school phobic children have a pathological fear of leaving mother, and difficulties within the school are irrelevant. Following on from this is the idea that removal from the family is the best way of overcoming this problem.

Although it is undoubtedly the case that stress of any kind within the family can affect the child's interaction in the school setting, to ignore the school setting, to ignore the school's negative aspects is stupid. Bullying and intimidation can have very adverse effects on sensitive children. (It also affects the children who are not so sensitive, in a different way. They grow up to be adults who believe that bullying is an essential part of growing up, to be accepted, instead of believing that this unpleasant form of behaviour should be changed). They also grow up liable to bully their own children and, the men, to bully their wives.

There are factors within the family which can affect the child's schooling. Bereavement and parental divorce are the most obvious. After either of these traumatic events, it should be possible for a child to be educated out of school for as long a period as the child wishes.

There is also the possibility that there is faulty mother-child bonding. The mother should not be blamed, as such a situation can be caused by circumstances outside her control. The policy of maternity hospitals, which separate new born babies from their mothers immediately after birth, as when the baby is born prematurely can drastically effect the mother-child bond, as can the policy of feeding babies on a strict 4-hourly schedule which can be very distressing for babies who do not fit into this routine.

The schools' psychiatric team, with their policy of

removing the child from the setting of the home, on the grounds that they are removing the child from a "pathological" environment, are acting on a mistaken premise. To educate a child out of school can be a therapeutic activity, during which time a bond may be formed between mother and child, where there was none before. The bond thus formed is perhaps never as well formed as it would have been if it had been formed in infancy, but at least some of the damage is repaired.

There is, of course, the possibility that an "overprotective" mother would become more so, if she were educating her child out of school. However, those that claim that this would happen have not realized that home education can, itself, be therapeutic, forging more adult and less repressive links between the mother and child. The LEA's official, visiting the parent could stress the importance of a child's learning to swim, for example, or joining a club of some sort, so that the mother would feel that she should delegate some of the responsibility.

A.   Negative Factors in school, as Precipitating Causes

1. Corporal punishment

Although corporal punishment in state schools has been abolished by Act of Parliament (Britain) in 1986, to take effect from 1987, I will keep this section substantially as it was written before that date, as the effects of corporal punishment will remain with the generation of children who were brought up under this regime; and, at the time of writing, it is still legal in private schools.

There are several negative aspects of school which have an effect on both truancy and school phobia. The most important has been corporal punishment. This is legalized bullying and is therefore a model of all other bullying that

86

takes place in and around the school. Legalized bullying teaches an aggressive/power relation towards a fearful/weak recipient. The recipients, in turn, carry the strong, aggressor – weak, oppressed relation to another situation where they themselves may be in power.

The power game goes something like this: teacher canes or hits child; child goes outside into playground and bullies a smaller child, either physically or verbally; smaller child goes home and is unpleasant to younger sibling, and therefore incurs the wrath of mother, who may inflict further corporal punishment, thus making a bad situation worse.

An alternative version of the power game is: teacher canes child, angry child on the way home from school, picks up a stone and uses it to smash a window. In this version, it can seem that there may be a direct link between corporal punishment and vandalism.

STOPP (Society of Teachers Opposed to Physical Punishment) gives examples of children who have suffered actual bodily harm as a result of a beating by a teacher; of children whose jaws have been broken, or who have suffered damage to the ear causing deafness as a result of a teacher's slap. If such a thing happened in the home as a result of a parent's beating, the child would be removed from the parent and taken into care. Teachers, however, tend to be acquitted and to continue teaching.

The Children's Legal Centre published the following case in their magazine 'Childright' in 1986.

For the first time the Criminal Injuries Compensation Board has awarded damages – an interim payment of £200 – to a pupil injured by a teacher. A 15 year old boy was summoned out of his classroom by the woodwork teacher and received injuries to his neck and windpipe described by his family doctor as "compatible with being forcibly grabbed around the neck". The teacher accepted a formal warning from the police. The boy's father was himself prosecuted for assaulting the teacher – he hit the teacher after hearing the extent of his son's injuries. The boy's father was fined £250 with £35 costs.

STOPP comments, 'The police were guilty of appalling double standards in prosecuting the boy's father but not the teacher. It now seems that, due only to the Criminal Injuries Compensation Board, the family will finally get some justice, after 18 months of waiting.'

There has not been a case of a teacher flogging a child to death since the 19th century in this country, when a child was flogged for such a length of time that he eventually died. ('A last resort?' by Peter Newell).

Unfortunately, a case has occurred quite recently in another part of the world, where an education system based upon the British system has been built up.

STOPP, 1985, reports the following:-

Seven year old beaten to death by teacher

The Zimbabwe Herald reported in March:

'A schoolboy, aged seven, died after he was beaten by his mathematics teacher for giving the wrong answer, Harare Regional Court heard yesterday. The teacher, Rossie Mtambanbagwe... denied an allegation of culpable homicide.

'The state alleges that Mtambanbagwe severely beat Kennedy Mutambirwa with a stick...... after he gave a wrong answer to a question about some work he had been taught. The boy died from a brain haemorrhage eight days later.

'A post-mortem report attributed the hemorrhage

to a 'bleeding disorder caused by about ten blows to the body using a stick or similar object'.

'Mtambanbugwe admitted striking the boy on the head, arms and legs with a light cane, but denied using excessive force or striking more than ten blows. She told the court that she was surprised when the boy was brought to her four days after the incident with severe bruising and swelling. She suggested that he was the type of person who bruises easily.

'The boy's father told the court that...... he saw his son with swellings on his arms and legs, and bruises on his head. The boy was bleeding from the mouth, he said.'

I am surprised and dismayed by a recent report from STOPP, stating that Church schools are among those least inclined to abandon corporal punishment. For the followers of Him who said that it would be "better for him that a millstone should be hanged about the neck of a person and he be drowned", rather than that he hurt a child, this is an amazing decision.

Corporal punishment can cause neurosis in the witnesses of the act as the following account shows:-

"When I reached early adulthood, my fear of men and the attendant anxieties, due presumably to a conflict between my feelings and my biological needs, were so intense that I was occasionally incapacitated and had sick leave for 'anxiety states' I needed twelve months psychotherapy to overcome this fear of sex that I have learnt in the primary school.

"When I was a little girl, the boys in the primary school were caned. This taught me the lesson that boys are nasty rough creatures who could only be controlled by caning. Fear of men was aggravated by the fact that the cane was wielded by a man.

"At that time, in the early 1940's, sewerage and water had not yet reached our village. To reach our very primitive lavatories, the girls had to pass the boy's lavatories, where the boys lay in wait to spray us with urine.

"A combination of these factors set the ideal stage for the development of a neurosis."

The effects of corporal punishment and bullying can last a lifetime, creating people who batter wives and children, and it can result in horrific crime.

'A man who ended up murdering his wife had been pushed off to boarding school at an early age; and been badly bullied by fellow pupils. When he reacted by stealing, starting fires and playing truant, he was beaten by staff' – Guardian, June 1984.

Parents, especially mothers, often understand how damaging corporal punishment can be, but making a stand against it can cause further problems, as in the following:

'A mother who kept her two teenage boys away from school in protest against their being caned was threatened by a mid-Glamorgan Council with a care order' – The Daily Telegraph, July 1984.

2. Intimidation of child by teacher

This is verbal bullying which may be used by a teacher as a form of control. Sarcasm on its own is sufficient to make a sensitive child feel really hurt. Occasionally it may be used in conjunction with a physical grabbing of the child. In one of the instances in this book, an already sensitive and frightened child was grabbed at the neck by a teacher. What was the crime, which deserved such rough handling? The child had failed to have a space in his book. The action of that particular teacher precipitated long-lasting school phobia.

One child says "Bullying by children is bad enough. Bullying by teachers is much worse."

3. Bullying

Bullying in the playground is one of the worst things a timid child has to endure. Very many children who do not go to school, both school phobic and truant, give bullying as the chief reason for their dislike.

Starting with the legalized bullying found in the headmaster's office, and continuing with the theories of developmental psychologists, bullying is accepted as a part of life. For teenage children to go through a period when they gang together in groups of one sex or the other is considered perfectly normal. The male gang is typically aggressive, bullying and full of bravado. The female gang usually limits its bullying to verbal bullying – spite.

The structure of adolescent peer groups is now considered so much a normal part of development that it has been accepted by developmental psychologists and psychiatrists as being the normal way to develop. Any child who is timid and a loner is considered abnormal and, if he or she also develops school phobia, to be in need of psychiatric treatment. The psychologists should visit countries where the aggressive gang is not part of normal adolescent development and revise their theories.

The fact that psychologists and psychiatrists believe that it is normal to go through an aggressive, bullying stage gives official sanction to a most unpleasant and dangerous model of growth and development. It is dangerous for the social health of our nation. It also sanctions the scapegoating of timid, vulnerable children by professionals.

We have been brain-washed into believing that it is somehow "good for you" to learn how to withstand bullies, and that the lessons so learnt will be of benefit in adult life. Most adults take care to avoid bullies as far as possible so it is an unnecessary lesson to have learnt. This also results in another generation of children growing up in the belief that bullies are an unpleasant but "normal" part of life.

The Metropolitan Police estimate that 4300 children run away to London each year. The London Teenage Project, whose workers befriend such children, say that very many children run away from home because they are afraid of school bullies.

After having completed his fifth form studies and successfully passed his O Level exams, a 16 year old boy started in the sixth form. On the first day in the sixth form he was attacked in the playground by a boy with a knife. His attacker only used his fists, but threatened to use the knife if the boy returned his blows.

By the time his attacker desisted, the boy was in a very sorry state. The headmaster told him to sit in a room by himself in the school, and he was not seen by either a doctor or a nurse, nor were his parents informed. The boy asked to be allowed to go home but this was refused until about three hours after the incident. He was then allowed to walk the two miles home without being accompanied.

Fortunately for him, a friend of the family gave the boy a lift home.

When his parents came home they immediately phoned the headmaster and then took the boy to the doctor. As a result of his injuries, the boy was unable to go to school for a whole week.

As a result of the family's complaints, both to the school and to the police, there was a court case a few weeks later. It was of course a juvenile court and therefore received no publicity. The lack of publicity of a juvenile court is ostensibly to protect the child, but in this instance it served to protect the school and the headmaster.

The boy did not become school phobic but after a few months in the sixth form, decided to discontinue his studies without completing the course.

> 'A schoolboy who had been bullied daily for four years, knifed a friend to death in an "inexplicable explosion of violence". Guardian, Oct. 1982

> 'A 14 year old boy ran away to Ireland to escape bullying at school. It took him 18 months to pluck up courage to return home.' Daily Telegraph, May 1984.

> 'School bullies have claimed another victim. A 14 year old at Bedales top public school hanged himself rather than face any more of their cruel taunts and pranks. His death highlights a problem common to all schools, for children can be unbelievably nasty to their schoolmates, particularly if they stand out from the crowd in any way. Experts estimate that for a staggering 400,000 children in British schools, everyday life is a misery of sly assaults or cruel jokes.' Daily Express, 1985.

Malcolm

During his primary school years, Malcolm was a happy little child. This changed shortly after the move to the secondary school. About seven weeks after he had started at the large comprehensive school, Malcolm's mother was contacted by the school and asked to take her boy home. He had been taken ill.

"The school had also contacted the hospital but, fortunately I got there before the ambulance. Goodness knows what would have happened if he had been taken to hospital." When his mother collected him he was sickly white and had severe stomach pains. The school suspected it was appendicitis.

His mother took him immediately to the local doctor who seemed unconcerned. He said it was probably caused by a virus and that Malcolm would be better in a couple of days.

After two days, the pain subsided but Malcolm was still obviously unwell, "like a walking zombie" said his mother. She returned to the doctor who said that Malcolm was fit to return to school.

Then the nightmare began. When they had returned home and he was told to collect his school things for the next day, he became quite hysterical, and ran round and round screaming "You're trying to get me now. You're trying to kill me. Leave me alone, I am choking." It was a nervous breakdown. During the breakdown he couldn't laugh or smile; he looked as though he was dying; after his hysterical outburst, he became very quiet and his time clock reversed. He slept all day and paced round the house at night. Often he would ask to sleep with his parents, he was so frightened.

What had caused this? Over the next few weeks, his parents found out some of the things which had happened at school and which could have precipitated a nervous breakdown. One day, on the school bus, an older boy had pulled Malcolm's school tie so tightly that he thought that he was being throttled. Later, the same boy threatened to beat him up in the playground. A few days after this, Malcolm became lost inside the enormous school, unable to find his way to his own classroom. A combination of the three had been sufficient to trigger off a breakdown.

94

A few weeks later, the family was asked to see two social workers, as Malcolm was not attending school. "One of them said she was a magistrate and if we did not send Malcolm to school we could find ourselves the subject of a care order." The other social worker suggested that Malcolm was possibly subnormal. "I was livid" said his mother, "I told them he just had a phobia about school."

After that there was a time of seeing endless doctors, paediatricians, and psychologists.

At the time of being seen by the paediatrician, he received about ten skull X-rays without parent's permission. Later, the paediatrician said words to the effect of "As far as I am concerned, you don't exist. You have never been a patient of mine, and never will be, and I never want to see you again."

They decided that perhaps a small private school would be the answer, so they went to see a small school nearby.

"When we arrived there, he was curled up on the back seat. He started to cry and scream "Please, please don't make me, Mum. I'll do anything, but please take me away from here."

Visits from the education officials to the home continued. One official told mother that one of the ways they tried to get school phobic children to school was to visit a school for handicapped children. "That way", he said, "they can see how lucky they are not having to be locked up like that." Malcolm's mother was aghast. What a dreadful thing, to put handicapped children on display like that.

As the family started to consider having a home tutor, Malcolm at last reverted to his usual cheerful self. He even offered to sell all of his toys to pay for a tutor. As he worked with the tutor he became once more the intelligent and happy child he had been before. He was certainly not subnormal!

At one time Malcolm's mother managed to see the report written by the social worker, psychiatrist, etc. It was full of inaccuracies, contained distortions of the truth as well as untruths. "If we had been taken to court and a magistrate had seen it, he would have been taken into care. I have no doubt about that. Our family was described in thoroughly disagreeable terms."

Malcolm has now saved enough pocket money to buy a donkey for which he takes full responsibility.

When he had a new bike he said, "I am not restricted any more. I need not stay around the village. I can widen my horizons now." And mother had been accused of preventing her child from venturing from home!

4. The stress of overcrowding

Our comprehensive schools are too big. Both the incidence of truancy and that of school phobia increase dramatically at the age of 12 or 13, at the time of transfer to large depersonalised schools, indicating that there is a minority of children who find such large numbers of people to be intolerably stressful.

Research into the stressful effects of mass production techniques has shown that stress is decreased when work is done in small groups. Although such research has been carried out in the workplace, the similar effect of very large schools on children has scarcely been considered.

In Denmark, the "small schools" flourish, each school being supported by a Government grant, but in this country there is no equivalent Government supported scheme. Instead, virtually all the State Education funds at secondary level are directed to very large comprehensives.

For those who fail to fit into the Government supported schemes there is a proliferation of schools for the "maladjusted". I would ask the question, how many so-called "maladjusted" children would prove to be perfectly normal if we did not try to fit them into such an abnormal environment as a large school for a long period of their youth?

Many of the parents who have written to me on the subject of school phobia have said that their children are afraid to go where there are "people". The so-called "socialising" effect of school can actually work in a negative manner, creating persons who are afraid of other people.

I was a school "success", that is, I left school with a handful of O level exams and a couple of A levels, and went on to further education. But I was frightened of people. I found the large numbers of people in school to be an extremely stressful situation, had frequent and recurring nightmares about being a very small person trapped in the middle of a crowd of very much larger people, and spent my days in school struggling, like an overwhelmed swimmer, to keep my head above water.

I have spent my adult life trying to overcome the fear of people which I learnt in that environment.

The stress of overcrowding has been studied in laboratory animals. Mice cease to breed under severely overcrowded conditions, rabbits re-absorb their embryos. Humans, however, continue to live in overcrowded surroundings, and to build up stressful environments in their cities; and to follow this policy in the education of their young, who are crowded together in enormous schools.

5. Communal nakedness.

Robert Wilkins, a child psychiatrist, writing in the Guardian, June 1986, draws attention to the fact that all the children he has encountered in the course of his work, dislike communal showers after games. He has questioned normal children as well as those who are emotionally disturbed.

He says, 'Every day in our schools children are expected to become physically fit in ways which put their mental health in great danger. I refer, of course, to communal showers.

'Compulsory group nakedness constitutes a gross

infringement upon the civil liberties of a child, and is a prospect no adult would willingly contemplate, evoking, as it does rememberances of army recruitment centres or, more chillingly, the spectre of Nazi pogroms.

'In my secondary school, communal ablutions soon became inextricably linked in my mind with physical exercise, and my strong aversion to the former soon induced a loathing for the latter.'

Dr Wilkins says that the anxiety caused by communal showering can have many negative effects: it can cause a loathing for sport; school phobia or truancy; erosion of self esteem; and long-term problems of sexual inadequacy.

6. Sexual assault by headmaster

It is to be hoped that it is extremely rare. I know of one occasion where this has occurred, and the incident caused the little girl in question to develop disturbed behaviour and school phobia. She was assessed by the schools' psychiatric team without parental consent and labelled "maladjusted". No one in authority would believe the little girl's story. According to the psychiatric team, it was a figment of the girls imagination, her "sick" imagination. I would say, what child at the age of eight would be able to invent such a story?

This strikes me as being very similar to Freud's reaction when he found that many of the neurotic women he was treating had been sexually molested when children, and which is quoted by Paula Caplan in her book 'The Myth Of Women's Masochism'. Instead of admitting it was the sexual assault that underlay the neurosis, what did he do? He invented the "Oedipus complex" and applied neurotic motives not only to neurotic women, but to all children. According to this theory, the women in his study had not been sexually assaulted, but had only had fantasies of being sexually molested by their fathers when they were children, and therefore all children, he said, at the age of about three, have sexual fantasies with the parent of the other sex.

This has been exposed by Jeffrey Masson who has had access to the unpublished works on Freud. His book 'Assault On Truth: Freud's Suppression Of The Seduction Theory' reads like a detective story.

To support this theory, Freud tells of little Hans. According to Freud, the story of Little Hans provides proof of the theory of the Oedipus complex. The little boy, aged about five, had developed a phobia about horses. This, Freud said, symbolized Hans' fear of his father's revenge because he, Hans, desired his mother, sexually. Freud completely ignored the explanation given by the little boy, that he had become afraid of horses when he saw a horse, harnessed to a horse bus, fall down. This is short summary of an article in 'Critical Essays In Psychoanalysis' by Stanley Rachman, which is a book written for professionals. A more popular account has been written by Eysenck, 'Decline And Fall Of The Freudian Empire'.

B.   Precipitating causes. Attributes of the child.

There are several attributes of a child which, because they make the child open to ridicule, make life very difficult for a child and thus predisposes towards school phobia and possibly also towards truancy.

1. Stammering

A child who stammers badly can have his or her life made a misery by other children in the playground who tease unmercifully. The effects of this are aggravated if an unsympathetic teacher asks a stammerer to speak in class.

This is the worst case of a stammering child that I have heard. This concerns a girl who found the stress of school so intolerable that her stammer became progressively worse and worse, until she lost her power of speech. She is now out of school but her mother tells me she is unable to do anything approaching the nature of school work or she loses her power of speech once more. Provided a relaxed atmosphere is maintained, the child is reasonably fluent in her speech.

Her mother is overcome with negative emotions, feelings of failure, guilt, isolation and fear.

Peter

Peter has a stammer, and was of course, teased in school. He coped reasonably well with school until the second year of the comprehensive at which time he started getting stomach aches which kept him away from school. These were miraculously better in the holidays, but even during the holidays he would not go out to play.

During the last two weeks of the summer holidays, his stammer started getting worse. Eventually he became very weepy and told his parents that he was teased, bullied and laughed at for stammering

In September, he started a new form with an unpleasant form teacher. She asked his name and he couldn't say it. Amid laughter from the class, he was told by the teacher not to be misbehave. When he came home after school, he lay down on his bed and wept.

The teachers were then asked not to ask him to speak in the class. Some of the teachers did not get the message and he was sometimes asked questions in the class. When this happened, he went to pieces again.

In November, after teasing and verbal abuse, he walked out of school and walked all the way to his mother's place of work. That was the last time he went to that school. He was by now on the verge of a nervous breakdown.

They saw the education psychologist who tried,

unsuccessfully, to use hypnosis on Peter.

Later, they saw the psychiatrist who asked questions about the family, but never asked about the school situation. He told the family to be aggressive towards Peter, so that he could learn to be aggressive in return. At the next visit, the psychiatrist started talking about care orders. Mother felt shattered after this meeting.

At this time, mother discovered that home education is possible. As soon as home education was started, there was a dramatic change in the child. He was educated out of school for one year, after which time he decided to go back to school. He now attends a smaller comprehensive and is coping well.

2. Dyslexia

When I was a student teacher, visiting a school for the first time, I came across a child, a six year old, who wrote a whole sentence in mirror writing. I was interested, but made no comment to the child except to praise him for his good work. At the end of the lesson, the teacher came bustling in, saw his work and said "What do you mean by all this untidy scribbling?" The poor little child! He had probably worked for about 20 minutes to produce that piece of writing, and had not realised it went backwards. I wonder how many times such things were said to him and how it affected his self-confidence. The difficulty of dyslexia had not been realised at that time.

Although I do not know what happened to that particular child, I do know the outcome in the case of some other children.

Henry

When Henry was born, his mother was in labour for 16

hours and it was a forceps delivery. He was a crying baby, always crying, which put considerable pressure on the mother who was depressed and at her wits end. The mother-child bond was not developing optimally under these conditions. As a result of this he became a child who never wanted a cuddle. He was rejecting what mother offered.

When first introduced to nursery school, he was upset by the numbers of children and sat with his coat over his head on many mornings. It was not until two months had passed that he decided to stay at nursery school. For quite a time after this he only watched other children playing, but eventually he decided to join in, and really enjoyed it.

When he started infant school, he was ridiculed by the teacher for his mirror writing. (It turned out that he was dyslexic). As a result of being ridiculed, he became disruptive. Mother asked to see the educational psychologist because of Henry's disruptive behaviour. This was refused.

At the age of eight, Mother took him to a private educational psychologist. It was now that the dyslexia was diagnosed. He then went to the Dyslexia Unit for 18 months, during which time he caught up two and a half years of schooling.

Because of his learning difficulties he was always kept in a class with younger children. The children teased him, called him "Brain Damaged" and "Mental". He has walked out of school many, many times and has truanted frequently in the comprehensive school.

All this has put considerable stress on the parent's marriage.

At the time when he attended the Child Guidance Clinic, mother did not realize until afterwards that whatever the psychologist said was only making him worse. They never had any advice from the psychiatric team.

His parents found a smaller secondary school, but things seemed to go from bad to worse.

His parents have been trying to get him into a situation

102

where he is taught in a small group. At the age of 13 he was having two hours in a small, special unit at school. His maths level was about age eight and his English level was about age ten.

He has a very low self-image. "I am nothing, I want to die". He made little cuts on his face with a razor blade, "I don't care. No one likes me." He has difficulty in making friends, but goes around with a group. Although his parents are non-smokers, he started smoking when he was twelve "I don't care if I get cancer".

When Henry was interviewed by the psychologist, Year Head and Deputy Head to find out why he dislikes school, his mother was labelled as being "overprotective and fussy". The ridicule and cruel teasing he had received were regarded by the experts as being quite irrelevant.

Nov. 1985. A "formal assessment" is being made on Henry. His parents are hopeful that mainstream schooling will be recommended as wrong. They are convinced that the large group of a comprehensive is bad for him.

While the results of the assessment are being awaited, he goes to school for one hour twice a week for remedial English. But he is afraid of meeting people, so mother takes him to the school when the corridors are empty.

Philip

There was a crisis early on in Philip's life. When he was three and a half his elder sister spent some time in hospital and, as his mother spent time in the hospital with his sister, he consequently felt rejected. Then at the age of five, just as he was starting school, his beloved Grandfather, who lived in the same house, died.

He has a dyslexic problem and often wrote in mirror writing. Starting from this time in the infant school, he was ridiculed by teachers, in front of the whole class, for his writing. At the age of five he was kept in at playtime and made to sit facing the wall. His self-confidence plummeted. The teachers called him "lazy", presumably because it took him such a long time to manage to write correctly. At the age of eight he was made to take his work, to show all the teachers his "terrible writing". The teacher encouraged the other children to call him "lazy". The headmaster forbade him from going on a school trip because he was not doing enough work.

As a result of the victimisation and ridicule, he was very unhappy at the primary school and the change to the comprehensive school proved to be the last straw. On the first day at this school, the form teacher caught him and held him by the neck, for not leaving a space on the page. He was waylayed in corridors by a bully. The headmaster did nothing to stop this.

School phobia set in at eleven and a half. He had no confidence in himself, and often said he wished he were dead; he had stomach pains, sickness and nightmares. He dreamt that he hadn't finished some work and the teacher started hitting him and wouldn't stop.

They saw both the educational psychologist and the child psychiatrist. They gave no advice, and said, "Let Philip go to school by train instead of by car." To Philip, the psychologist said "You will be all excited when you see the train coming in, and you'll get on with the other children and have a nice train journey to school. "He is far too intelligent a child to be swept along like a sheep with the other children.

Mother asked if Philip could go into a remedial class, not because he needed remedial teaching, but because it was a smaller unit, separate from the rest of the school.

On the first day in the remedial group, the teachers were very nice. Mother was allowed to stay outside the classroom on the first and second days. Philip sat near the open door so that he could see his mother.

On the third day, mother said to Philip "I will stay in the

104

car outside while you run into school very quickly without looking back", so he ran into school. He was back almost immediately, sobbing. The head of the remedial group had caught hold of him and given him a row for running in school.

After that, the parents employed a private psychologist. He found Philip to have a high IQ, and to have dyslexic problems. This was the first time dyslexia had been diagnosed.

They were taken to court for non-attendance at school. The case was adjourned. After the second court hearing, the case was dropped.

Both Philip and his sister were educated at home for one year and eight months and the family was left alone. The school refused to de-register them.

During this time he became a different boy. He regained his confidence, no longer hated himself and was no longer ill.

After one year eight months the Local Education Authority started harassing the family again. The children were not doing enough work, they said. No allowance was made for the fact that Philip finds great difficulty in writing and was working to his limit.

The LEA wanted the children to attend the "adjustment class" in the Psychological centre. (The LEA presumably receives a grant for each child who attends.) They started in the school phobic unit in September when Philip was 13 and his sister was 15. They settled well in this small class with ten children of different ages.

In January, the children's other Grandfather died. Both children were very upset.

At Easter, the elder sister will be leaving school to start a course in childcare. Philip is now very worried about staying at the centre without his sister.

He has started having nightmares again, about his best

friend dying.

He cries again for long periods, saying his writing is no good, that he is no use. The teacher that he has at present has not complained of his writing, but the others in the past have said it to him so many times that this is how it has left him.

According to the Dyslexic Institute, 4% of the population are dyslexic. They may be distinguished from other people by involuntary eye movements which make their perception different from the other 96% of the population.

> 'A new computerised test which works by tracking the involuntary eye movements of dyslexic children has been hailed as a major diagnostic breakthrough....... Many dyslexic children, through constant academic failure and low self-esteem, develop an aversion to school before they are properly diagnosed....... Edward is one of the 4% of the school population estimated to suffer from severe dyslexia – otherwise known as "specific learning difficulties". He is also one of the thousands to have been written off as "lazy" because schools and local education authorities have been either unable or unwilling to recognise this disorder'. The Times Educational Supplement, Oct. 1986.

The computerised test may be used on very young children, enabling them to be diagnosed and given remedial help before they have experienced the humiliation of being unable to learn to read, which leads to their being called "lazy" and results in loss of self-confidence. However, many more children than the 4% may be labelled as "dyslexic". I have seen articles written, in which it was stated that 20% of children are dyslexic. This is nonsense. Inability to read can result from several different causes: it can result from extreme unhappiness of a child due, perhaps, to bereavement; it can result from poor teaching; and it can result from too much pressure to learn to read being put on the child before he or she has reached what is known as "reading readiness". It can also result from anxiety.

From my experience as an infant teacher, I am well aware that the majority of children do not reach what is termed "reading readiness" until the age of six or six and a half. This means that for many children, they will have been in school for perhaps one and a half years or more before they reach the the point at which they can learn to read. During this time, many children may have had pressure put on them to read, either at school or at home. This can be counter-productive, creating such anxiety in a child that he or she becomes unable to read.

In Steiner schools, it is the policy never to teach any child to read until the age of seven, at which age, most of the children learn quickly.

In all other countries, children do not go to school at least until the age of six. It would be interesting to compare the literacy rate in a country such as Denmark, where children do not go to school until the age of seven, with that of our own country. I suspect that it might be much higher, due solely to the fact that no child is expected to be able to read before the age of seven, and children have not become discouraged and lost their self-confidence at an early age.

3. Left Handedness

Left handedness should never cause any problems. Any problem so caused has been entirely the fault of an infant teacher who has forced the child to write with his or her right hand. For a left-handed person, control of the right hand is very difficult, and attempts to write result in what looks to the teacher like scribbling. The child is then punished for scribbling. If this has happened to a child who is also dyslexic, the effect is magnified.

Roland

Roland was born with slight brain damage resulting in learning difficulties which were apparent before he started school. His development in both walking and talking was slow.

He started school at the age of four and a half. His teacher forced him to use his right hand when he was naturally left handed. This, added to the fact that he had dyslexic problems and tended to write mirror writing, led to what was labelled "scribbling" by the teacher. When the class watched television programmes, Roland was left in a room on his own, as punishment for "scribbling". He was only four and a half.

From this time on, he lost his self-confidence. All through the infant school he lost more and more confidence.

At the age of seven he was assigned to a special school. At first he went to a school for maladjusted children. It was disastrous for such a timid, quiet child to be placed in a class with disruptive and unruly children. He became more and more withdrawn.

Then, for a period, he went to an "Enrichment Unit", which was very good. Here he learnt many practical crafts, swimming, etc. and he learnt to read. The Enrichment Unit's course was of short duration, only two terms. At the end of the two terms when his confidence had been considerably restored, the problem again arose. What school should he go to?

For a time, mother taught him at home. Since he had learning difficulties associated with dyslexia, a great deal of time was spent in reading and writing practice.

Then, once again, the search for schools was on. They had

exhausted the possibilities of the state system, so now they visited private schools up and down the country, to see if they could find a suitable school. They visited many schools: schools where the pupils were unruly and disruptive; one school where all the children were drugged; and one or two which just might be possible, but were far from ideal.

It was at this point in time, when Roland was approaching eleven, that the family decided to move to Australia. There they were lucky. Although the state system could again provide nothing suitable, the family found a very friendly, small alternative school run by Quakers. Here Roland has been happy for three years, but his self-confidence is still very low, as a result of his experiences in the infant and junior schools.

C.   Bereavement and other Family Trauma

1. Bereavement

It is a recognised fact that it can take an adult person between one and two years to recover from a bereavement. However, children are expected to return to school immediately, as though nothing has happened. It seems incredible to me that this should be so.

Anyone with a modicum of common sense can understand that a shock of this nature could precipitate severe disturbance in a child. However, psychiatrists and other members of the schools' psychiatric team, are blinded by the theory of separation anxiety. They, the "caring" profession, completely ignore the effects of grief. As usual, it is mother who is blamed, for being "overprotective".

Children, severely shocked by a bereavement, unable to work through their grief, unable to face school in their present condition, are then threatened with court cases and care orders. To hold the threat of removal from home and family over a child who is already in mourning is extremely inhumane and insensitive.

Not all children who have suffered a bereavement become school refusers. I know a child who lost her mother at the age of five, just at the age when she started school. She spent her time in school being sad; just sitting quietly and being sad. She did not learn anything; for years she learnt nothing. Fortunately for this particular child, after a few years she had a new stepmother who taught her to read at the age of nine.

In a humane society, we would say to a child who has suffered a bereavement, "I know you feel terrible. Would you like to do your schoolwork at home, until you are ready to cope with school again?" We should allow a child to continue his or her learning at home for just as long as he or she wishes. There should be no pressure to return to school at any particular time.

It is also necessary to be aware that the death of a pet can sometimes affect a child almost as badly as the death of a human.

Julie

When she was ten years old, Julie found the dead body of a friend in the garden. The shock was so great that it precipated school phobia. She became extremely unhappy in school, started developing mysterious illnesses and had frequent nightmares.

The headmaster was unsympathetic and said it was a relationship problem between mother and child, and that there was no trouble at school.

Julie was not forced to go to school during the last term of primary school.

Her mother was very relieved to find that she started secondary school quite happily. By the third term, however, troubles had started again. Julie suffered from headaches, vomiting attacks, high temperatures, etc. and attended school only spasmodically.

Mother phoned the school to explain the difficulties. The Education Welfare Officer arrived, and shouted so loudly that mother was frightened. He told mother that she must force Julie to school, manhandling her into the car if necessary. As Julie was dragged into EWO's car, she kicked, bit, scratched and screamed.

The EWO called regularly to force the child to school, and with threats of court cases and care orders, insisting that mother should drag the child to school each morning.

Mother was by now in a state of depression. The relationship between mother and child deteriorated. Julie became withdrawn, sullen and rude, alienating herself from the rest of the family. As tensions rose to an intolerable level within the family Julie's two elder sisters, both college students, spent less and less time at home. The whole family was disintegrating.

The family had a meeting with two psychiatrists. (There was a one-way mirror in the room and they discovered afterwards that there were three other officials behind the mirror).

At this meeting, the psychiatrists completely ignored the traumatic effect of finding the dead body, and said that the whole trouble was caused because the mother was weak. Mother was already in a depressed state because of the situation. The last thing she needed was to be told she was inadequate, especially when her three children were there.

Mother tried the "hard line" with Julie for a week. Julie locked herself in the bathroom.

The EWO said he was instigating court proceedings and would recommend a care order, "and then you will lose her for six years". This is intimidation of the parent.

By now Julie walked about looking like a zombie and had made a suicide threat. The family was falling apart.

Mother phoned the Citizens Advice Bureau who told her that no one could put a child into care without a Social Worker's report.

The Social Worker arrived with the idea of manhandling Julie to school, but after a couple of attempts when Julie was locked in the bathroom said, "Sod it, let's have a cup of coffee"

The authorities then decided to work out a "package" for Julie at a case conference (mother understood that this would be a home tutor, followed by gradual re-introduction to classes a few mornings a week, and finally going to school full time when her confidence was restored).

In August, mother was invited to a case conference. When she arrived, she found it had already occurred, and was handed a slip of paper which contained the decision of the conference, which was to put Julie into "voluntary" care. She would be put into a children's home and forced to go to the same school as before. If she co-operated, she would be allowed home at weekends. Mother was horrified. When she was asked to sign the "contract", she refused.

The officials then decided that mother was trying to undermine the authorities and said that if Julie was not in school by the first week in September, she would be taken to court and a compulsory care order put on her.

Mother was shattered, but she had just heard of Education Otherwise, so she de-registered the child from school and employed two tutors. Once Julie was told that she would be home educated, would not have to go to school, would not be taken into care, her behaviour became normal and she stopped looking like a zombie, she is now co-operative and happy.

During the year when Julie was away from school there had been case conferences to which mother was invited. At these meetings, the EWO distorted facts and even told downright lies. Also, mother, said that she, herself, was treated like a moron.

The Use of Drugs Following a Bereavement

A ten year old girl's sister and her husband were killed in a car crash. The shock precipitated school phobia and, for a time, she was given a home tutor. After a few months, however, she was told she must return to school. She was to be drugged to enforce this.

Fortunately, at this point, the family discovered that it is possible to educate a child out of school.

2. Divorce

A divorce can have effects similar to a bereavement, the effects are especially severe if it occurs at the age of school entry.

Ken

His mother had a difficult delivery, and was depressed for some time after Ken's birth, and was treated with antidepressants. Her husband was away at this time.

Perhaps the maternal depression prevented the formation of optimal mother-child bond. The parents' marriage broke up when when Ken was five years old, triggering behaviour problems. If repremanded, he would break toys, etc. This coincided with the start of the school days.

At school he learnt nothing. He could not read at the age of seven. At this time his IQ was assessed by a private psychologist as 113, giving a mental age of nine and a half. In spite of this, the school was not worried by his inability to read. When mother had obtained this information about his mental age, she taught him to read in two or three weeks.

Mother sometimes had to take him forcibly to school at this time.

Until the age of nine and a half, Ken had good contact

with his father. At this time, contact virtually stopped. He then refused school totally and developed severe behaviour problems. After one or two days at home, he would be forcibly taken to school by his mother. He was suicidal and violent and seen by Child Guidance, but it was no help.

He was later seen by the educational psychologist who said he was depressed and that if he did not want to go to school, he need not go. There was no suggestion of alternative education.

After two years mother suggested to father that he start seeing Ken and his sister again. Ken's behaviour settled. There were no more school problems or behaviour disturbance for a year or so, until they moved house.

At the time of moving house, Ken and his sister went to stay with their father and his new wife for one month. Ken was desperately unhappy because the wife made it obvious that the children were not welcome.

The children then returned home to a new house, new town, new friends and new school. Ken hated the comprehensive school from the very first day, although his sister liked her school. After half term, Ken started refusing to go to school. At first he was taken by his mother, but eventually he refused to go at all. Pressure from his mother to attend was of no avail.

Mother took him to the G.P. in December. By the beginning of January when his behaviour was reverting to its former disturbed pattern, he was referred to the educational psychologist, who had limited success in getting Ken to school; this was followed by eventual failure.

They then applied for a transfer of schools. At the interview at the new school, he was interested, but the interest was not maintained when he started there. He was bored, had done the work before, also he was accused of cheating, etc.

The family then asked the LEA for another change of schools. This was refused, as the other school was out of the

114

catchment area.

There was now a total breakdown of Ken's behaviour. He was suicidal, violent, bizarre, paranoid, absent minded, semi-comatosed at times, depressed and hysterical at other times.

Appointments were made to see the child psychiatrist. Mother went, alone, to the first appointment because Ken refused to come. She was told to bring Ken next time.

Ken saw the psychiatrist on the second occasion. The following day his behaviour became completely disturbed. He took a hammer and went round the house smashing windows, etc. He smashed the computer. Then he rushed into the kitchen, found a bottle of paracetamol medicine which he tipped down his throat. Mother had phoned the police during the episode. The police arrived and took Ken to hospital because of the overdose of paracetamol. He was discharged from hospital the following day.

Mother had meanwhile contacted Ken's father to say that he was in hospital; and father arrived on that day, also.

Two days later Ken saw the psychiatrist at the (third) appointment made the previous week, together with his father and mother. He was offered a place as a day patient in the psychiatric unit in two week's time.

He became more settled as it was now Easter time and he was officially on holiday, but his behaviour was still rather strange, and he would not go where there were "people". He went away for a two week holiday and was more relaxed, but still not himself.

He returned on April 14th, the day before he was due to start at the unit, and started smashing windows again.

The next day, Monday, Ken refused to go to the unit. Mother phoned the psychiatrist who was unable to help. Mother then phoned the G.P. who visited, and diagnosed severe depression. The G.P. said that he would phone the psychiatrist.

A phone call came from the G.P. at lunchtime. The psychiatrist said that if mother would volunteer Ken into care, the social services would get him to the unit. Reluctantly, mother did this. The social workers refused to take voluntary care, as they said that they could not get him psychiatric help. It was not their job.

Tuesday: The Social worker spoke to the psychiatrist.

Thursday: The psychiatrist came to see Ken. He saw Ken first, then his mother. The psychiatrist told mother that there was nothing wrong with Ken, that he was just an arrogant child with power over his mother, that he was not suicidal, and that his violent behaviour was only tantrums. Mother and the family were at fault and the only remedy was to remove Ken from mother. Mother told the psychiatrist that she disagreed. (There were two GP's in the practise who thought that Ken was depressed; also several relatives, who were also doctors, agreed that he needed help for depression)

A friend suggested that mother should get a second opinion and suggested a doctor – Dr A – in a nearby town. Mother obtained the appointment with Dr A, but the social worker sneered.

They managed to keep the appointment. Mother and daughter were asked to see the Registrar first. Ken was left outside the room. Suddenly, mother looked up and she could see Ken running away, outside the window. She caught up with him with the car and brought him back. He refused to get out of the car, so the nurses took over. Mother went back to the doctor, feeling "absolutely shattered".

Then Ken went in to see the doctor. A residential place was offered to him; but not for some time.

During the preceding months, mother had asked both the

school and the LEA for school work for Ken to do at home. This was refused.

Not knowing how long they would have to wait for a place at the residential unit, the Senior Schools Medical Officer wrote to the LEA to ask for a home tutor. This was also refused.

May 12th. Mother went into hospital for a minor operation, father had meanwhile come to look after the children.

May 13th. A letter arrived, saying that Ken would be admitted to the unit on the following day.

May 14th. On the way to the unit, Ken got out of the car and ran away. Mother asked the social worker for help. This was refused.

May 15th. Mother asked to see the leader of the social workers at the hospital, who said that they would be able to help. The social worker provided a car and escort for Ken the following day. Ken himself was not told about this arrangement until immediately before they left.

There was difficulty in getting Ken into the unit but, once there, he settled quickly and appeared happy in the unit school with only 16 pupils of mixed ages. He was happy to be learning again in this small group.

After only one month in this environment in which he could learn properly, he was transferred back to the comprehensive school whilst still resident at the unit.

A week later there was a parents' evening. Mother arrived (knowing from phone calls that Ken had run away every day, had not slept, had cut his arms with broken glass, etc.). She asked why Ken had been taken out of the unit school when it was the only education he had received that year. She was told that they "had been led to believe that there was no problem" and also that he should return to the comprehensive, as he was "not behind for his age".

In the following six weeks, Ken went to school a few

times. He attended only about five classes. He developed asthma, broke the door, window locks and rubbish bins. He ran off almost every day.

Mother was blamed by the doctor. It is all mother's fault. "You encourage him not to go to school. You let the children do as they like. You have a confusing relationship with your ex-husband. You rely on the social services too much. Why can you not manage? Other single parents can manage".

Mother is, incidentally, a professional woman used to coping with other people's problems.

The only suggestion that this doctor could offer was to threaten Ken with a care order. With this threat hanging over him, he just might go to school.

It was at this point that mother discovered Education Otherwise and that it is possible to educate a child out of school. Once the pressure of school was removed, merely by talking about the possibility of home education, Ken started behaving normally.

He now works happily at home, using correspondence courses

3. Birth Trauma

Akin to the effect of bereavement can be the effect of birth-trauma leading to the non-formation of the mother-child bond. I was first put on this train of thought by reading 'Suicidal behaviour in Children' by R. Kosky. In his study of suicidal children, he finds that 65% have had difficulties at birth, leading to a subsequent troubled childhood with many behaviour problems. He postulates that difficulties at birth may have "an adverse effect on the formation of the mother-child bond." He finds a similar number of the suicidal children to be from families in which there is considerable marital stress. Unfortunately, he gives no indication whether there is any correlation between the trauma at birth with its tendency to lead to disturbed childhood behaviour, and the marital stress of parents.

The number of children in Kosky's study is of necessity very small, as he is concerned only with suicidal behaviour before the age of 14. These form a very small percentage of the child suicide attempts.

Is the marital stress antecedent to or subsequent to the emergence of a troubled child? Is it parental disharmony which causes the child to develop a suicidal response? Or is it a troubled child within the family caused by birth trauma (for example), which causes the marital stress? I suspect the latter.

Controlled studies into the effect of separating newborn babies from their mothers have been carried out by Garrow and Smith; and by Jeffcoate, Humphrey and Lloyd. The results were similar in both cases.

'Evidence is accumulating to show that separating a baby from its mother may have unhappy, even disastrous effects.' A high proportion of the children in the separated group, in both studies, developed psychological, psychosomatic and psychosocial problems in later childhood. The researchers found no difference between these babies and the control group at the age of six months. The effects of the early separation were latent at this age, only to become evident later on in childhood. It is this group, of children who were separated from their mothers after birth and who have subsequently developed an unsatisfactory relationship with the mother, which provides the statistics of "battered babies."

Garrow and Smith further noted that "such disturbances seem to have repercussions on other members of the family." In one of the families in their study, the parents sought marriage guidance, due to the stress of the relations created within the family. They quote other studies where the troubles of the children have had such severe

119

repercussions on several families that the parents were divorced.

We, the parents, are so often blamed for circumstances outside our control.

Several parents who have corresponded with me have told me that having a troubled child in their midst has put considerable stress on family relations. Is it the negative emotions caused by having a troubled child in the midst of the family that are picked up by the child psychiatrist and labelled "separation anxiety?"

"Behaviour problems following assaults (by teacher) were severe and prolonged, did and does affect the marriage. The child psychiatrist maintained that there was nothing wrong with him, and it was all to do with the parents (by then coping with five years of a disturbed child had led to a really rocky marriage)."

"My son's attitudes have come very close to making both my husband and me want to leave home and be without him. He is very difficult to deal with, and seems to have a self-destruct button which he pushes frequently."

"The situation is causing a great deal of tension now, not only for my son, but also for the rest of the family".

In another family, all the nine years of getting their child to school have been a nightmare. The effects on other members of the family have been devastating. The elder sister's O Level exams were affected because she could not cope with the turmoil in the house. She failed two exams. Mother's health was affected. She developed high blood pressure due to stress which resulted in a near stroke and she spent some time in hospital as a result. Father's health has also been affected. He suffers from tinnitus (ringing in the ears) which is made worse by tension, and he needed treatment with tranquillizers.

The child even asked that she might be sent into care, because she knew she was upsetting the family so much.

At one time she tried shoplifting.

At the age of fourteen and a half, she made a suicide attempt: an overdose of drugs. After this, the family discovered it was possible to educate a child out of school, and made moves to de-register her from school.

Ruth

After a prolonged labour, and drugged with pethidin to keep down her blood pressure, mother gave birth to a five pound baby. The baby was immediately whisked off and placed in an incubator for 24 hours while mother lay in a drugged stupor, sleeping off the effects of the pethidin.

When the 24 hours were up, the baby was brought to mother for feeding. She was so small that she was able to suckle for no more than a minute or two before she fell asleep. She was also probably affected by the drug which mother had received to control her blood pressure, and which can cause not only the mother, but also the baby to be sleepy. Long before the next feeding was due, mother could hear her screaming in the nursery. However, the baby had to be "disciplined" to a four hourly feeding schedule. Mother's blood pressure was still awry, leaving her very dizzy, so she was completely unable to walk to the nursery, to go to the baby herself, and was wholly dependant upon the nurses.

When the baby was bought to her at the end of the regulation four hours, the baby fell asleep, exhausted from so much crying, after only one or two minutes of feeding. Once again she had had insufficient food to last for four hours, and the cycle was repeated.

Each time she was brought for a feeding, the baby was already exhausted from crying, and fell asleep before she had had sufficient. Mother asked to be allowed to feed the baby on demand. This was refused as was the request to be discharged from hospital. (Mother was very upset about this as she had, on two occasions during her antenatal visits, asked for a 48 hour discharge. The request was now refused

121

on the grounds that she had not asked the consultant – he had not been at the hospital on the two occasions when she made her request). She was feeling too weak to take the law into her own hands and discharge herself.

After five days had passed, the medical staff discovered that the baby had not regained her birth weight, so her mother was asked to feed her on demand.

As a result of this treatment, the mother-baby bond was not formed. Did it also cause the mother's post natal depression? Did the depression set in as a result of hearing the baby cry for long periods at a time, and being unable to do anything about it?

For the sake of the convenience of a four hourly routine imposed upon the babies in the first week of life, damage had been done to this particular child, the effects of which would last for many years. Why had a four hourly routine been imposed on this baby? Did it really make for convenience to the nursing staff, to have a baby who cried incessantly for long periods?

By the time they left the hospital, the damage was done. A pattern of frequent and prolonged crying had set in. She cried for several hours in the evening and again for two hours in the middle of every night. This pattern of behaviour lasted for at least nine months. Mother's depression lasted for about twelve months.

The pattern of crying behaviour gradually merged into behaviour problems of the toddler. By the time she was three years old, these behaviour problems were evident: tantrums, soiling, bedwetting, nightmares. Ruth's mother says "Any parent has to cope with a few tantrums; but five every day, each lasting for about half an hour. Two and a half hours of tantrums every day! Very wearying for me, and very wearying for the child. In addition, there were nightmares practically every night. However, when she was not having a tantrum, she was a very active and appealing child."

At this time, mother also had all the extra laundry caused by the bedwetting and the soiling, and she was also coping with a new baby. Mother's life at this time was one long round of broken nights, laundry and tantrums. She was always tired. All those troubles put considerable strain on the marriage.

The behaviour problems were so severe that mother sought help from the Child Guidance clinic. The therapist said that Ruth was afraid that mother would die. That the child was indeed afraid of death is illustrated by the following events:-

> When a bunch of daffodils died and had to be thrown in the bin, it precipitated a tantrum. "The daffodils are dead! The daffodils are dead!" she screamed. The next morning, shortly after she awoke she had yet another tantrum screaming, "The daffodils are dead".

All through her toddlerhood, the little girl played with a group of seven children who ranged from a few weeks to a few months older than herself, but those few weeks were vital. The whole group attended nursery school together for one year and then, in September, all but Ruth started at school. She was too young. She no longer went happily to nursery school. Instead she went to nursery school rather frightened. She told her mother that all her friends were dead.

Her fear that mother was dead had probably arisen, said the therapist, as a direct result of being left to cry for long periods in the hospital in the first week of life. The mother-child bond is such an important relationship that great care should be taken in maternity hospitals to ensure that nothing will damage its formation.

The therapy they received at the Child Guidance Clinic (twice a week for two and a half years) solved the outward problems of tantrums, soiling, etc., and relations between mother and child were calmer than they had been, but the relationship problem remained to some extent, a source of sadness to mother. She could never be totally relaxed with Ruth.

The atmosphere remained strained between mother and daughter for many years. This was a great source of sadness to the mother who had always been very fond of children, and was now unable to be relaxed with her own eldest child.

"I won't go back to school next term". This was Ruth's statement uttered several times during the summer holidays, after the first year at the comprehensive school. Mother ignored this, and hoped for the best.

On the last day of the holiday, after having given virtually no help in the kitchen for the whole of the holiday, Ruth suddenly set to and produced a delicious curry for supper. The following day, she lay in bed, groaning "Fatty foods always disagree with me."

The next day she also lay in bed. And the next! Whatever was the matter? Mother began to panic.

Mother had realized that there was something wrong several months earlier, when money started disappearing from her hand-bag, and later, when Ruth made friends with the naughtiest girl in school.

From now on, she went to school occasionally. Also, she never smiled; never smiled in months!

Mother's most obvious feeling was, why should this happen to me?

It was not until two years later that Ruth told her mother one of the circumstances which had made school so difficult.

It was the inter-school sports day. A coach load of children from each of the competing schools converged on a sports field, remote from any buildings except a small pavilion. It rained for six hours. The children arrived home absolutely drenched.

The headmaster never even wrote a letter of apology to the parents concerned. When Ruth's mother made a complaint, he said hers was the only complaint he had ever received, and went on to pass the blame to others: to the sports organizer who had arranged the outing, and to the meteorological office for giving an incorrect forecast. There was still no apology.

As a result of her mother's complaint, the gym teacher was told to talk to Ruth. She was taken by the gym teacher who gave her a "good talking to." "Why did you complain about the school?" "You should never complain about the school." "Don't ever do it again." She talked to the poor, frightened child in this manner for 30 minutes. (Ruth had not complained, it was her mother who did so.)

It was after this occasion that her health deteriorated, and her attendance became spasmodic.

After a little while, the child psychiatrist and the education psychologist were called in. Mother and child had two or three interviews with these officials, at first quite relaxed on the adult's part, but very tense on the part of Ruth who still never smiled. At the third interview with the psychiatrist, his attitude changed dramatically. He was abrupt and aggressive. Mother was very upset by this change in attitude. (Later, she was thankful that she had been present, and that Ruth had not had to cope with this herself). "You must go back to school", he said. Mother pointed out that her non-smiling daughter was by now making suicidal threats. These, the psychiatrist ignored, as frivolous and meaningless remarks, empty threats. Presumably he knew the suicide statistics; mother didn't at the time. If mother had followed the psychiatrist's advice, would she have her daughter now?

The psychiatrist's advice to force her back to school (he could arrange for the welfare-officer, polite term for "truancy officer", to forcibly take her to school every morning), had been based only on an investigation of the strains and stresses of interpersonal relationships within the family. He never asked about the school situation which had been the actual cause of the crisis.

Trained in modern psychiatric thought, the psychiatrist presumably saw "separation anxiety" in the family. According to the theory developed about school phobia, some children, aged perhaps twelve or thirteen suddenly develop an unnatural fear of leaving mum. This is reciprocated by a similar fear on the part of the mother, unable to part from her child. On analysing her emotions at that time, Ruth's mother finds the following:-

1. The mother-child relationship problem, which had been caused by trauma at birth, and which had led to so many behaviour problems in early childhood.
2. Mother's sadness because of the relationship difficulty.
3. Marital stress resulting in large part from the effects of the primary stress
4. Worry and anxiety on the part of both parents as a result of the behaviour of their daughter.
5. Guilt, which is always felt by the parents of a suicidal child.
6. Fear that Ruth might actually carry out her threat.

It is this complex of negative emotions that the psychiatrist sees and labels "separation anxiety." Neither of the parents was afraid of parting from their child. The child, far from being afraid of parting from mum, felt she wanted to run away from home.

Although mother is a trained teacher and had expressed her desire to teach her child at home, the psychiatrist tried to dissuade her, telling her that the child would never learn to socialise, indeed, he said that she would grow up with so little ability to socialise, that she would never get married! (If mother had not felt completely dumbfounded by this remark – or was it a threat? – she would have replied that, of course, her child would not get married if she had committed suicide). This is emotional blackmail.

Mother left this interview feeling shattered, and longing for a cup of coffee. How she managed to drive home, she never knew. She also never knew how her child felt; her daughter never spoke, and when she arrived home, locked herself in her bedroom.

Mother was at first very doubtful of her ability to teach Ruth at home, because of the relationship problem which had been between them for so long; mother's self-confidence was shattered, and she was overcome by negative emotions.

She was unprepared for the surprise. Once the pressure to go to school had been lifted, the mother-child relationship problem which had always been present, gradually diminished and finally disappeared. Two years later, mother and child were relaxed together as they had never been before. This, at the age of when many teenagers are rebelling against their parents!

Ruth has been highly motivated to do her studying at home because she knew that she would otherwise have to go to school.

She had been afraid of her peer group at school. It was not until she had been out of school for 18 months that she began to socialise with her friends in the village, again. It was a slow but real process, far more real than any socialising that would have occurred if she had been forced back to school. Since her parents waited for her to be ready, instead of forcing her into the school environment, she has been able to overcome her fears.

Her comment, on first entering technical college, where she socializes well, was, "Nobody humiliates us like they did at school.

As a postscript to this story, mother says she wishes the baby had been born at home where she would have been able to feed her at any time the baby wished; and, in retrospect, she wonders if having the baby in bed with her, instead of in a cot, would have averted the trouble of the childhood behaviour problems and, if this had been the case, how it would have affected the later development of her child.

She was given to understand that babies should be born in hospital, to keep the perinatal death rate low as possible. (Her GP gave her no choice in the matter.) However, in Holland, where it is the norm for babies to be born at home, the perinatal death rate is as low as it is in this country.

The Effects of a Series of Crises in One Child's Life

The arrival of the baby, and the mother's subsequent postnatal depression may have speeded up the rift in these parents' already unhappy marriage. The marriage broke up when the child was two, triggering behaviour problems.

Mother works in a children's nursery and, until the age of two and a half, the child had accompanied his mother to work. At this time a new ruling at the nursery meant that he could no longer be accepted in the same nursery, but had to attend a different one. No alternative place could be found for his brother who was six weeks old, so the baby continued to accompany his mother.

This ruling, which was for the convenience of the staff and took no thought of the consequences upon the children concerned, had very grave effects on this particular child. This, again, is an example of a circumstance completely out of the mother's control which has severe consequences on the behaviour and development of the child. The mother will be blamed for his disruptive and aggressive behaviour, and it will be added to the statistics of the single parent family.

Shortly after his baby brother was born, the baby had to spend eight weeks in hospital. Mother naturally spent more time in hospital with the baby than she did with the elder boy.

When the little boy was three, two significant things happened. There was a new man in mother's life, and the little boy started at nursery school. These triggered many behaviour problems: aggressiveness and shouting in the nursery school; he threatens to kill his mother and wishes he were dead. This saddens me very much: suicidal wishes in a child of three, triggered off by nursery school.

When the mother wrote to me, the child was six, and both mother and child had been seeing a private therapist for one and a half years.

At the age of five, just when he started school, the father-figure left. These two events, occurring simultaneously, triggered even more behaviour problems. When he was six, mother discovered that it is possible to educate a child out of school, and was considering doing this. I hope she succeeded and that it has had a beneficial effect on the little boy.

This is an example of true separation anxiety, caused by circumstances outside the mother's control. However, the mother will be blamed, and labelled as "overprotective" or "colluding".

Several parents have written to me that their child's trouble began in the nursery school at the age of three. Almost ten per cent of the letters I have received have told of school phobia developing at the age of three as a result of forcing an unwilling child to nursery school.

It is right that Health Visitors should recommend nursery school as a socializing and mind-expanding environment for three and four year olds, and there should be an adequate provision of nursery schools. But all parents should be warned that, if their child does not settle immediately, he/she should wait until he/she is older. Damage can be done to very young children separated from their mother or mother figure before they have reached the emotional stage to do so. This stage is not reached at the same age in all children, and it is often reached much later in children who have been through some crisis early on in life.

129

Adequate provision of nursery schools, which can also be used as community centres, where parents are invited in for a cup of tea and a chat, is urgently needed in areas of social deprivation, especially the inner city areas of decay and recent riots. If children from the local schools were also included in such a scheme, each child being expected to help in a nursery school as part of their education, a wide range of people in the area would be helped by such a scheme, which would give school children first hand experience of childcare.

In Russian schools, all children are expected to spend part of their schooldays in a state nursery or playgroup, learning to handle small children and babies (Bronfenbrenner). Such a policy should help the next generation of parents and their children.

If we introduced such a policy in this country, so that all children, both boys and girls, spent perhaps two weeks helping in a play group, nursery school or baby clinic, several times during their schooldays, every child should develop a greater awareness of how to relate to small children; and a generation of young adults would grow up with more understanding and responsibility towards their children. In this way, we might even be able to eliminate the "problem family", the family with irresponsible and non-caring parents, in one generation.

It is quite ludicrous that parentcraft should be an optional school subject chosen mainly by non-academic girls. This should be part of the core curriculum for both boys and girls. The knowledge gained in such a course could help future parents to prevent alienation between generations which is so common in our society.

Suicidal Behaviour

Under the title 'Epitaph for Hirofumi', the Guardian, March 1986, tells of a child in Japan who was beaten with a

130

toy wooden sword for 30 minutes by a group of bullies at school. Shortly afterwards he hanged himself. The suicide rate of children and young people in Japan is very high. In 1984, 62 children under the age of 14 committed suicide in Japan, and 572 young people under the age of 19 did so.

The equivalent rates in Britain during 1983 were two and 84. The Samaritans tell me that in 1985 in Britain, an estimated 200,000 people made suicide attempts.

Japanese educators are extremely worried about the level of bullying in their schools which leads to such tragic results. Japanese classes are very large, their discipline extremely strict and the academic pressure is high.

The suicide rate among young people in Britain is lower, but on the increase, and for every completed suicide there are many more suicide attempts.

'Deaths from suicide are likely to be under-reported to a marked extent so that official suicide statistics fail to represent the true incidence of suicide in England and Wales, a verdict of "accidental death' or "undetermined causes" is often reached... the number of officially recorded suicides among children under 15 years of age is small. When undetermined deaths and accidental deaths due to poisoning are considered, a different picture emerges, suggesting that there may have been an increase in suicides in this age group which is not revealed by the official suicide statistics.

'McClure examined deaths classified as undetermined or accidental due to poisoning. He found that in the ten to 14 age group there had been a very marked increase in deaths in these categories between 1951 and 1980, the increase being five-fold when the decades 1951-1960 and 1971-1980 were compared. There has also been an increase in deaths in these categories among 15 to 19 year olds, especially girls.' (from 'Suicide And Attempted Suicide Among Children And Adolescents' by Keith Hawton.)

As an example of an obvious suicide being reported as accidental, I include an article from the Daily Express. The tragedy here is not, as the coroner decided, that she did not mean to kill herself. She obviously did. The tragedy is that her act was not taken as being serious.

TRUANT TRAGEDY

Teenager Who Hated School Found Hanged

'A shy teenager hanged herself because she hated school, an inquest heard today.

'But tragically, the girl, Tanya Dixit, 16, did not intend to kill herself. "It seemed more like a cry for help," said the deputy coroner at Hornsey, North London.

Tanya Dixit, who forged her mother's name on sick notes, had only been to school for eight or nine days during the Autumn term.

'Mrs Dixit told the inquest, "Tanya was very unhappy at school and kept pleading with me not to go.

'"I am convinced she did this because she wanted to prove how much she hated school."

'Mrs Dixit discovered her daughter's body hanging from a stair bannister at their home in North London.

Tanya was still alive, but died two hours later in intensive care in hospital.

'Miss F., Tanya's teacher, said she put her absence down to the fact that Tanya suffered from asthma.

'Miss F. added, "She was shy and didn't have many friends, but I had no indication she was so unhappy. I never saw the girls taunting her."

'Police found a note in Tanya's bedroom to her mother saying, I'm sorry for signing absentee notes in your name saying I was ill."

'The coroner said, "The note does not indicate she wanted to kill herself."

'The pathologist agreed: "The circumstances surrounding this case are more in keeping with a half-hearted attempt."

'Verdict: Open.' The Daily Express, January 1987

A suicide act is not a cry for help, it is a cry of despair. I share the view of Moses Laufer in his book 'Adolescent Disturbance And Breakdown'. To call a suicide attempt a cry for help is to trivialize it. To say that a drug overdose or a self-inflicted injury is of "low suicidal intent" is not to hear the message which is that life (including school) is intolerable.

The girl in the article has already tried a cry for help. She has pleaded with her mother that she should not go to school. Since her mother did not know her rights under Section 36 of the Education Act, she insisted that the child continue in school. At last, in desperation, and with added guilt that she had been forging her mother's name, she took her life. As a last act she wrote to her mother apologizing for forging her name. Owing to the fact that the note did not include her intention, the death is not recorded as suicide.

It saddens me that these children's voices are not heard. If we acknowledged the true extent of suicides and attempted suicides, we would have to admit to grave failings in the educational system and in the social provision for children and especially adolescents.

How many young lives must be lost before the silent cry is heard?

Why was Tanya's mother never told that it was legal to educate her child out of school? Has her death been in vain? Or will parents in the future be told of the "Otherwise" option in education? Will there be a move towards smaller schools where the individual will not be lost in the crowd?

Our society tends to stigmatize and ostracize the families in which a child suicide has occurred. How tragic. We compound the agony of a family already in mourning.

Like myself, Moses Laufer ('Adolescent Disturbance And Breakdown') and Sally O'Brien ('The Negative Scream') consider that every suicidal attempt is serious and, at the time, the person wishes to die. Attempts to take one's life are cries of despair, not cries for help, and the classification of suicides and suicide attempts as being "cries of help" or "attention seeking devices" is a classification within the minds of professionals, not the reality, and such labelling prevents us seeking for the malaise within our society which causes such despair.

The Samaritans say that a suicide threat should never be ignored, but educational psychologists and child psychiatrists, working in the schools' psychiatric team, regularly tell parents to ignore a child's suicide threat. Suicide attempts by children are considered by these specialists to be "attention-seeking devices". A suicide attempt is not. It is a cry of despair.

Any parent who has not experienced it, cannot visualize what it is like to hear a child say "I will kill myself if you make me go back to school." No wonder the psychiatrists sees anxiety in the families of school phobic children, but it is not "separation anxiety".

No-one without such an experience can imagine the fear with which mother opens the bedroom door to wake her child up in the morning. She is fearful that the suicide threat may have been carried out.

Suicidal behaviour is a potential killer, and yet we are told to ignore the threats!

According to the Samaritans 750/100,000 teenagers between the ages 15 and 19 now attempt suicide. If a child or young person makes a suicide attempt, there is a 4% chance that that person will succeed in killing himself or herself in the next ten years. After two attempts, there is a 10% chance that he or she will be dead in the next 10 years. In a recent study at Edinburgh University (1979) of teenagers between the ages 15 and 19, more than one per cent of the girls made a suicide attempt each year. Fewer boys made an attempt but, because boys tend to choose more violent methods, more boys succeed in killing themselves.

With statistics like these. why are we told to ignore suicide threats?

'Look Now' magazine carried out a survey of 2,000 teenage girls and young women. According to their finding, 10% of the girls between 15 and 17 had made a suicide attempt, and many more had thought of the possibility. (Quoted in the Daily Post, April 1986).

From the Daily Telegraph, June 1983 – 'A "shy" 13 year old hanged herself because she hated school.'

Clare

Clare was born by caesarian section at eight months. She was a very small baby, and was put in an incubator for several weeks. Later on in her infancy, she was hospitalized with bronchitis. These traumatic events in early life probably prevented optimal formation of the mother-child bond, and made her susceptible to depression.

She was obviously a bright child and developed an interest in books before her second birthday.

She disliked school from the very beginning. Her parents

moved around a great deal, so there were very many different schools in Clare's life, in England, Scotland, France and New Zealand. In all she went to between 20 and 30 different schools. Every time she moved, there was the trauma of having to leave friends and make a new set of friends.

When the family moved to France, the necessity of learning French was added to the stress of adjusting to new schools. Although her attendance was poor, she put great pressure on herself to learn the new language and do well academically. She succeeded in learning French so well that her thought processes were in that language and she had to translate back into English in order to talk to her parents.

At every school she went to, in whatever country, the story was the same. After two or three weeks, she started suffering from tummy upsets and stayed away from school. Her mother tried everything to get her to return to school. She screamed at her, spanked her and eventually gave her work to do at home. Because of her interest in books, this was no hardship at all for Clare. Most of her learning was done at home as she suffered so badly from tummy upsets, and also constant crying.

She was taken to doctors in all the different places she lived, and they all prescribed medicines which Clare thinks must have been sugar water, for all the effect they had.

The turmoil produced in the family by her fear of school, all the screaming and crying, caused a great deal of trouble in family relationships. Her parents eventually divorced when she was ten years old; no doubt the stress caused by Clare's difficulties had been one of the contributory causes.

After attending several schools in Britain, the family moved to France. Her second school in France was in Nice. It was here, at the age of eight, she first felt suicidal. She felt under terrible pressure and found herself wishing to die. She climbed a wall which was two or three times her height, and decided that if she jumped off it, she would probably be

136

killed. When she jumped off, she landed with such a jolt that she had a choking feeling but, apart from that, she was only scratched. She never told anyone about it.

That was the first of several suicide attempts during the next seven years.

After her parents' divorce when she was ten years old, she lived in New Zealand with her mother. By now her thinking was in French and she had to re-learn English almost as if it were a foreign language.

At the age of twelve, a social worker was assigned to her. She had become very quiet and withdrawn, and wouldn't talk to people; she sulked and hated many things; she shouted and cried easily when under pressure; and many were the times when she locked herself in the toilet. Then she became a compulsive eater, and put on three stones in weight.

Finally, she was going to be taken into care at the age of 14, for non-attendance at school.

She then decided that she would return to England and live with her Dad. He paid her fare for her to come over.

Once she started school again, this time in London, the same problems arose because of her shyness, quietness and her weight. She was an object of ridicule to her classmates. (She was 4ft. 9ins. high and weighed 13 stone 3 pounds).

One month after her 15th birthday, she again tried to end her life. This was followed by a nervous breakdown. She couldn't stop crying, had stomach pains and vomited. She didn't trust people, hated herself, and wanted to die. "I was becoming suicidal by the minute." She was taken to the psychiatric unit of London hospital.

The psychiatrist could find no reason for her breakdown. Clare knew what the trouble was, but was too scared to tell him. A nice lady came into the hospital to give lessons to Clare and some other children; but after three and half months, it was decided that Clare should return to her previous school. "I hate to tell you how terrible I felt.

Petrified is not a strong enough word, but I put on a good front to the doctors. They had no idea at this time."

She had to travel across London to her school. She cried between the hospital and the station. She cried on the tube train. In the end, she could not manage to go to school, and went home instead, still sobbing.

Her step-mother calmed her down and advised her to tell the doctor about her fears. This suggestion made Clare burst in to tears again. However, her step-mother insisted that psychiatrists are sympathetic people, trained to understand problems.

When she returned to the hospital, she acted on her mum's advise. She told the psychiatrist how frightened she was of school. His attitude changed immediately from being sympathetic. He became aggressive and spoke in a nasty tone: "Rubbish, There is no such thing as a phobia of school. You just hate school like many other children and you are just making an excuse not to go. Don't talk to me about it again."

The rapport that had been built up between herself and the psychiatrist dissolved in that instant. From then on, she had no trust in the medical staff.

On the next day, she started crying even before she started to put on her school uniform, and she cried all morning.

A short while later she returned home, intending to try to go to school again, but deep down inside herself, she knew she would not be able to.

It was at this time that her Grandfather died and she was naturally very upset.

She was left alone for a little while, but soon the Local Education Authority and the hospital authorities began putting pressure on her return to school. ("Pounced on me again" are the words she uses). In addition to her fear of school and her grief for her Grandad, she had now developed agoraphobia.

A psychiatric social worker was assigned to her and came to visit her at home on many occasions before she was able to overcome her fear of going outside.

The headmistress and the LEA official came to see her some time later and suggested that she join the remedial class. She agreed; but on the way there she had such a bad stomach ache and terrible fear that she returned home.

The social worker visited after a few days. The decision was made to try a tuition centre. This was the best decision that had ever been made with regard to her schooling. In the small group situation with a tutor, she was more relaxed than she had ever been in school. In this environment, she studied successfully for CSE examinations.

Robert Kosky found that some of the children in his study of suicide attempters had deliberately run out into heavy traffic in an attempt at suicide, and points to the probability that quite a proportion of road accidents are a result of suicide attempts. Clare's story indicates that there are children, some of the "accident prone" children who are, in actual fact, suicide attempters.

I will conclude this chapter with a quotation from 'The Politics of Experience' by R.D.Laing:

'A child born today in the United Kingdom stands ten times greater chance of being admitted to a mental hospital than to a university, and about one fifth of mental hospital admissions are diagnosed as schizophrenic. This can be taken as an indication that we are driving our children mad more effectively than we educating them. Perhaps it is our way of educating them that is driving them mad.'

CHAPTER EIGHT

Misuse of Public Money

When parents wish to educate a child at home, and approach a school asking for the child to be de-registered, they may or may not find it a simple matter. Difficulties may be raised by the school, supported by the Local Education Authority, refusing to de-register the child. There are a number of cases known to me, when the child is being educated out of school, but remains on the school register. The school is thus illegally claiming either £15 a week for a primary age child, or £22 a week for a secondary age child (1985 figures). Under these circumstances, a family, educating a child out of school in a perfectly efficient and satisfactory manner, is liable to be prosecuted under Section 39 of the Education Act, with expenditure of further public money. How much public money is involved in a court case? or in residential institutions of one type or another? Section 79 of the Education Act states that children be educated according to the wishes of their parents and "the avoidance of unnecessary public expenditure." How much unnecessary public expenditure has there been in the following case?

Derek and Daniel

When Derek and his younger brother Daniel were at primary school, they were both happy little children. There was no indication of the nightmare which was to begin a few years later.

After the transfer to the comprehensive school, at the age of twelve, Derek had a nervous breakdown with hysterical paralysis. This affected mainly his right leg, and for a time he could only move with a wheelchair. He was seen regularly by a psychiatrist for a period of three months, but visits to the psychiatrist seemed to make him even more depressed. He spent much of his time curled up in bed refusing to talk, he slept badly and was very unhappy.

He was doing his school work at home, now but, in his depressed state, was not performing well. The psychiatrist recommended either a residential school or inpatient treatment in a psychiatric unit.

When the psychiatrist told the family that this was school phobia, they joined Education Otherwise and talked about the possibility of home education. Derek was keen on the idea and started exercises to strengthen his leg, and started to get over the depression and black moods.

Derek was enrolled with a correspondence college and his parents asked the school to de-register him. The school refused to do this.

He started work with the correspondence course in September. He enjoyed the work and, apart from occasional short-lived depressions, was getting very fit. He had been afraid of meeting people during the past few months when his depression was severe. He now overcame this fear and enjoyed his hobby of radio-controlled cars.

In October, they were visited by a psychiatrist, Dr B., who said that Derek should be back in school, and offered him an outpatient appointment. The parents refused to accept this.

December. They were visited at home by the School Education Adviser Mr S. and the Education Welfare Officer (EWO).

January. They received a letter from the psychiatrist, Dr B, again saying that Derek should be in school. The parents replied that home education was going very well and that Derek was improving all the time.

Also in January, the parents were invited to see the educational psychologist, Mr C, in his office. This meeting had been arranged by the Education Adviser. The parents explained why they wanted to continue to educate Derek at home, and Mr C. seemed satisfied.

In March, Daniel awoke one morning, complaining of severe back pains. He was taken to the G.P. who said it was muscle strain. In the next three weeks he was seen by all members of the G.P. group who agreed he was in pain but could not agree on the cause. (He had fallen off his bike about nine months earlier, and hurt his back at that time. That had healed long ago, so there was probably no connection with his previous back trouble).

Daniel was taken to the hospital for X-rays, but nothing unusual was seen on the X-ray. The doctor who examined him said that the muscles were in spasm, but did not know the cause. The G.P. had sent the hospital a long letter telling of Derek's problems. After reading it, he said that the back trouble could possibly be due to psychological causes, and arranged an appointment with the child psychiatrist.

May. When Daniel was seen by the psychiatrist, the visit was very short as he had seen the G.P.'s letter about Derek, and had a preconceived idea that this was school phobia. He told Daniel that all his troubles were in his mind. Poor Daniel was very upset, he said "I'm not like Derek, but they want me to be." And, "Alright, if they want me to be school phobic, I will be."

Daniel was by now in such pain that he was confined to bed most of the time. His body was rigid, "as though it had been starched." His parents had to lift him out of bed like a wooden doll and carry him, for example, to the toilet. He could walk only a few steps, with the help of a walking stick which he held in front of him with both hands. The attempt to walk caused him great pain. Extraordinarily enough, being lifted or turned over in bed in a rigid state did not cause him much pain.

In June the parents were informed that there would be a case conference about the two boys. At the conference it was decided that Daniel was in too much pain to attend school, and that Dr W, the School Medical Officer should visit the family in the next week.

Dr W. visited the family the next week, took a complete history of the two boys, and then examined both boys. He pronounced Derek as 100% physically fit and "should be in school." He agreed that Daniel was in very great pain. He spent three and three quarter hours on the visit. His report of the visit later became part of an affidavit, and is full of inaccuracies.

For the following month, until the school holiday, a tutor came for three hours a week to work with Daniel. The parents supplemented this with some of his brother's correspondence course work

Daniel has a great many allergy problems, being allergic to dust, pollen, moulds, cats, dogs, birds, grass, etc. At this time he was taken by his parents to see an allergy specialist, (to see if his back problems could be caused by allergy.) The allergy specialist arranged for him to go for urgent tests in a children's hospital in another city

The tests proved negative and he was advised to have hydrapool therapy and psychological treatment. As both of these were available in their home town, they brought him home.

Despite many phone-calls to Dr W. asking for the hydrapool treatment, nothing was arranged. Dr W. does not believe in allergy specialists. (He says so in the affidavit).

In August, one month later, he was seen by the allergy specialist again. He suggested that they test Daniel for food allergies by fasting. The results seemed to show that Daniel is allergic to many foods. The specialist then suggested that Daniel should be put on a vitamin therapy. Vitamin A, Vitamin D, and Vitamin B complex in high doses was given. Under this treatment, Daniel made some signs of improvement but it was very slow.

In September, the school tutor restarted. Daniel again used some of his brother's correspondence course work, in addition to the time spent with the tutor.

Daniel was granted both a Mobility Allowance and an Attendance Allowance. The doctor who examined him for these allowances, said he thought the problem was clearly physical and not psychological.

October. Dr W. visited again, examined Daniel, said he did not think the vitamin tablets were helping, and advised them to be discontinued. No other help was offered.

November 21st. Dr W. visited again for five minutes, examined Daniel briefly for about three minutes and told his mother that there would be a Case Conference about the two boys on the 25th. Two days later a physiotherapist turned up, saying she has been asked to assess Daniel for the Case Conference.

November 25th. Both parents turned up, uninvited, to the Case Conference. They discovered that it was held behind locked doors, and they were excluded. They were asked to wait in the anteroom.

"I listened at the door" mother said, "And I couldn't believe what I was hearing; such terrible things were being said about our family." Statements were made during the conference, based on very distorted facts. Among other things they heard was one member of the conference saying, "What can we do to frighten this woman?"

At length the conference was over. The parents were told that both boys must return to school, (Daniel was still far from well) and that home education would no longer be allowed. The children were deemed "at risk" and would be put under a supervision order. A Place of Safety Order was threatened. A Place of Safety Order gives the authorities emergency powers to remove a child from battering parents when a child is at risk of being abused by his or her parents. It should be used under no other circumstances. It was a gross misuse of emergency powers, to use it in this case.

The suggestion was that the children should be removed from the parents and placed in a psychiatric unit. When the parents pointed out that this would precipitate another nervous breakdown for Derek, the psychiatrist said it probably would "but it would be better in the long run. Then he can be treated in the unit and after that he will go happily to school."

This is incredible. A psychiatrist is actually advising someone to be ill! It is equivalent to a doctor saying "Go ahead and break your leg. A spell in hospital will do you good."

The family had been thinking of moving house for some time. The turn events had taken made them decide to put the house up for sale the next day. They wanted to leave the scene of unpleasantness. Father stayed in the house while mother and the two boys went to stay with relatives.

The EWO contacted the Social Services who contacted the Police to say that they had gone. Dad was told to go to the Police Station and was then ordered to get the family back. The feeling that he got in the Police Station was that the Police themselves did not seem happy at being involved. Nevertheless, he was threatened with the inside of a police cell.

Immediately on their return home, they contacted their solicitor who told them the boys could not be taken into care without a Social Worker's report, and advised them to keep a record of everything that was said in all meetings with officialdom. Sure enough, after a day or two, came the visit of the Social Worker. This was the first of very many visits. On one occasion, the Social Worker stayed for three whole hours. On this first occasion, the Social Worker departed after one hour saying that he could see nothing wrong with the family and would report to the Case Conference, due to take place on the following day, that the family was a happy family, and that the boys appeared to be contented.

As a result of this Case Conference the boys were told to attend the psychiatric unit, as in-patients, for an undefined length of time. The Place of Safety Order was used as a threat

145

to enforce this. When the parents asked the Social Worker why this had happened, after he had been impressed with the way the family was functioning, he replied that the School Medical Officer had explained to the Conference that this was a malfunctioning family and that the boys were not developing normally. "The boys are too happy," he said, "At their age they should be rebelling".

Derek's psychiatrist was not present at the Conference, there was only a report from a psychiatrist who had never met either boy.

From then on a Social Worker visited the family every week, since the boys were registered as "At Risk". Hours and hours of the Social Worker's time were spent with the family, looking for a chink in their armour. The Social Worker's attitude was not consistent. On one occasion it might be full of praise, and on the next it might be condemning.

At one point, just before Christmas, the parents had an interview with the chief psychiatrist in the area. The parents were not subdued by his haughty manner, and he could not make them agree to his suggestion. ("No child comes into my unit under force. All are voluntary patients") After an unsuccessful attempt at brainwashing the parents into agreeing to allow the boys into the psychiatric unit, the psychiatrist just stalked out of the room, almost in mid-sentence. The parents were confused. Was this the end of the interview, or not? Should they stay there, or should they go home? In the end, they asked at the reception desk, and were told to go home.

The boys were still at home for Christmas, but due to enter the psychiatric unit during the second week in January. The threat of the Place of Safety Order was again being used to enforce this.

It was not the happiest Christmas the family had spent. All through the holidays they made their plans. If the boys were taken away, either into the unit or into care, they would sell their house and buy a smaller one, so that they would have a few thousand pounds to fight court battles.

During the first week in January, they visited the unit. This was a unit for adolescents with severe psychiatric disturbances.

At this unit, which they visited in the afternoon, the children do their schoolwork in the morning, and in the afternoon it is recreation time. They arrived when recreational activities were in progress; table tennis, snooker, chess, etc. Their most abiding impression was that, engaged in recreational activities, not one of the children smiled, and there was a very unpleasant food smell about the place.

After the visit, Derek's condition deteriorated. He started having "black moods" of depression which he had not had for twelve months. During the last two or three months his academic work deteriorated, with the stress of the situation. Now he consistently got B's for his work, where previously he had had A's.

While at the unit, the parents had asked about schoolwork. "No. The boys will not be able to continue with science. No. There will be no opportunities for computer studies, we only do the basics, here".

When the second week of January came, the boys did not enter the unit. A court case was now threatened.

To try and keep the authorities happy the family spent Daniel's disability allowance on employing two tutors, in addition to the correspondence courses. They were now spending £60 a week on the boys' home education.

By now they were considering informing the media, and getting their story splashed in the press. However, their solicitors disuaded them. The parents received a letter from the LEA in February urging them in the best interest of their sons "to send them to school or accept the offer of treatment in the psychiatric unit." In other words, if they go to school, they don't need psychiatric treatment!

They contacted MIND at this time (the Mental Health

Association). It was imperative that the boys be seen by a independent psychiatrist. The family needed desperately to have the report of an independent psychiatrist.

In early February, in the hope of finding a cure for Daniel's disability, they left the National Health Service and turned to alternative medicine. With the help of vitamin therapy and some additional minerals Daniel started to recover. He had been paralysed from the waist down for ten months. Ten weeks after the vitamin and homeopathic therapy had started he could run down the front drive. "Not a proper run" he said, "it's a bit wobbly". So it never had been school phobia, but a metabolic disturbance.

The Social Worker still turned up once a week. One day in April, the Social Worker came and said there would be a Case Conference about the two boys the next day, and saying that everything was fine and that all would go smoothly.

The next day, as a result of the Case Conference, the boys were made Wards of Court. Now, nothing could be done without the court's permission. They even had to inform the court when they went on holiday.

MIND had been unsuccessful in recommending a sympathetic child psychiatrist. Now it was even more important that they find an independent psychiatrist, although it would not be possible to have the boys assessed without first asking the Court's permission.

More frantic telephone calls. They rang up everyone they could think of, trying to find a sympathetic psychiatrist. At last they were successful, but they had spent over £100 on telephone calls.

One advantage of Wardship proceedings over an ordinary court case is that the family was sent a draft affidavit in the form of a 22 page report from the Medical Officer, Dr .W. together with letters from two psychiatrists. They were able to study the report and note its inconsistencies.

The report is badly spelt and inaccurate. It is written by a Medical Officer who saw Derek on only one occasion, twelve

148

months previously, at which time he pronounced him 100% physically fit, and who saw Daniel on three occasions, on the last occasion for less than five minutes. He saw Daniel only when he was still confined to his bed. He did not know that, by the time the Wardship proceedings were made, Daniel was 95% fit and learning to ride a bicycle again.

The report begins with a medical history of the two boys. Dr W. remarks that he is surprised that mother told him the medical history with both the children present in the room. (This is the first inaccuracy. Neither boy was in the room). Dr W. says that "Derek had no childhood illnesses, per say" [sic].

He then goes on to say that at the age of nine, Derek had a suntan and then developed boils. (Mother said "He went swimming and then developed boils"). Dr W. then decides that Derek had developed an allergy to "sola radiation" [sic]. Actually, it had been an allergy to chlorine in the swimming pool.

He then said that at the time Derek developed trouble with his leg, he was seen by the educational psychologist. Neither boy was at any time seen by an educational psychologist. At the time when Derek first had trouble with his leg and went to school only in the morning, doing his work in the library, Dr W. said he "refused to go upstairs". This should have read "he was unable to go upstairs". Later, he said "Derek rejected Dr F. the psychiatrist". This should have read "Dr F. discharged him".

Dr W. goes on to say that the fact that mother told him of Derek's rapid growth and the associated changes occurring at puberty and which took four months, was "very significant indeed", that she had inserted this irrelevance in the middle of the story. Mother tells me that she told Dr W. this fact in its chronological position in the story. The fact that it is disconnected from the rest of the story is beside the point.

"He was noticed to be rarely sitting with his head up and when I asked why, Derek said it was tension." This is supposed to be what Mother told Dr W. She never did.

Dr W. then examined Derek whom he found 100% physically fit.

After this Dr W. took Daniel's medical history. He says that Daniel was allergic to sunlight when an infant and therefore never went outside. This is false, his mother says. She has "loads of photographs to prove the contrary."

Much is made by Dr W. about the food fads which Daniel developed at the age of 18 months. (Very many children develop food fads at this age, and the less notice that is taken of such fads, the better). However, Dr W. is using the food fads in an effort to show that mother is an over-fussy and neurotic mother, as he is using the incorrect "fact" that the child was not allowed outside as an infant. Mother tells me that at all times he had a mixed but very limited diet. Dr W's report says that at one time he had nothing but carrots and crisps, and at another time "nothing but celery soup through a straw". Mother says that at no time did he have celery soup, and he never drank any soup at all though a straw.

"Celery soup though a straw" is so significant to Dr W. that he brings it up again later in the report as a means of denigrating mother.

(My own feeling is that if in fact a child did develop a fancy for celery soup through a straw, allow the child to drink the soup this way and the fad will soon pass. If, however, a great fuss is made, this will only cause tension between parents and child, which may develop into much greater troubles linked with food, later on – see section on Anorexia nervosa).

When talking of Daniel's back trouble, Dr W makes much of the fact that his parents took him to see an "Austiopath" [sic] immediately after his hospital examination, to try once again to show that his parents were over-protective. The fact was that he had been seen by the three doctors in the G.P. group, who disagreed on diagnosis, and the hospital doctor who said it was all psychological. They had had four different diagnoses, and were feeling confused, to say the least. "Besides", says mother, "why shouldn't we visit an osteopath who happens to be a friend of ours?"

Dr W. said that during this interview Derek kept on coming into the room to remind mother that it was time to tell Daniel to have his pills. Mother says this is untrue.

According to Dr W.'s report, mother had to force her G.P. to agree for Daniel to see an allergy specialist. That is not true. It was father who went to the G.P. with a mere request. Dr W. then goes on to say that he finds it very significant that mother had to force the G.P. to agree to this referral.

He then examined Daniel. He was lying flat on his back in his parents' bed, and clutching a walking stick. His mother picked him up, as rigid as a wooden doll, and placed him on the floor, to demonstrate his walking. He managed only six steps, holding the walking stick with both hands in front of him. Dr W. considers that it is extremely unusual that he was asked to examine Daniel in his parents' bedroom. (The reason for this is that Daniel's own bedroom is tiny).

On his second visit to Daniel a few months later, Dr W. again thinks it highly significant that Daniel is once more lying on his parent's bed, again clutching the walking stick. By this visit, under the vitamin therapy given by the allergy specialist, Daniel had improved to the extent that he could walk for ten minutes, holding on. As Daniel was suffering from severe stomach aches, Dr W. told him to discontinue the vitamins. (Dr W. does not believe in vitamin therapy).

Dr W's opinion is that Daniel's pain and extreme rigidity is wholly hysterical in origin and that he is imprisoned in the house by his parents and denied friends and a normal life.

Dr W. visited again two weeks later. He was in the house for a mere five minutes and said that Daniel was lying on a couch with his head flexed at right angles to his body, again holding the walking stick "as if this were an object from which he would not be separated". This is untrue. He was playing a computer game, had no walking stick, and his neck was not flexed.

In his report he says that he had a discussion with mother saying that Daniel needs a normal life, i.e., going to school with his peers; and that the life of both Daniel and Derek is abnormal and that he was seriously worried about the implications for the future. In actual fact he spent only five minutes in the house and it was therefore impossible for any discussions.

The following are Dr W.'s opinions: "Derek has been denied normal developmental relations with his peers that a normal school life would have given him. He has shown symptoms and signs in the past which indicated a severe psychological disturbance. It is my opinion that Derek requires intensive psychiatric treatment." (Since when is it normal to give "intensive psychiatric treatment" for a condition which is passed?).

His opinion concerning Daniel is that his illness is largely imaginary and that he is "a prisoner trapped in his own house"; that he is extremely immature and psychiatrically disturbed; and in need of "intensive psychiatric treatment".

When the boys were eventually taken to court, the judge decided that they should remain Wards of Court *in order to protect them from the excesses of the Education Authority,* They continue to be educated out of school.

The mind boggles at the thought of how much public money has been involved in the harassment of this one family, and one may wonder in how many other cases has public money been similarly misused.

It is difficult not to come to the conclusion that the salary of the psychiatrists is affected by the number of children in the psychiatric unit.

Costs of care

In 1980-81 the number of children in care for non-attendance at school was 4200, and the cost to the rate and tax-payer was approximately £30 million a year.

> 'Average costs of placing young offenders in various kinds of care in 1984-85 were: community homes with education £418 per week, observation and assessment centres £413 per week, other community homes £260 per week.' Childright, June 1986.

CHAPTER NINE

The Story of John

John was born into a caring family, very much a wanted child. As a toddler he was a very busy little person, too busy to eat very much. His mother, Mrs Smith, was happy to let him eat little bits of cheese, apple, etc. but the doctor said "He must learn to sit at the table properly with you, and eat proper meals."

He was always busy: building, drawing, jigsaws, dot-to-dot, library books. One of his specialities at this early age was to do jigsaws upside down. His tricycle was one of his most treasured possessions. He loved other children coming to the house but was nervous of going to other people's houses.

When he was three, the Health Visitor suggested playschool "to get him used to proper school." This is was a large group in a Church Hall. He was petrified. Although it was a well-run playgroup with paints, crafts, climbing frame and sand tray, he stood with his back to the wall on the first three mornings. Then on the fourth morning he screamed all morning. He never went there again.

After some months had elapsed, he went to a different nursery school. This had only twelve children in a private house. He loved it. He learnt to read at this nursery school at the age of four and was very excited about his new ability. He would find words he knew in newspapers, books, etc. It was funny to see him sitting in the middle of "The Times" pointing out "the" or "is". He also learnt some arithmetic at the nursery school. He could do tens and units. He was obviously a bright little boy.

He started infant school at five years old. In this school, the very young ones were allowed to do more or less what they liked during the first term, allowing them time to "settle in". John was "dumb struck". He spent most of the first term standing at the sand tray sifting sand through his fingers. He came home for lunch each day and wouldn't eat and wouldn't talk. He was a worried little boy.

The nice teacher was ill the second term and the class had a supply teacher who was not a trained infant teacher. She was fearsome. She made him use his right hand when he was naturally left handed. (This was found out many years later through hypnotherapy). As a result of this his work books were full of scribbles instead of the writing he had been capable of before this. Because his work had now deteriorated into scribbles the teacher used to stand him on the table as a punishment and say, "Isn't he a naughty boy?" The class had to chorus "Yes, Miss" (This was found out after it had continued every day for two terms).

During this time, John became more and more stunned. He stopped reading, writing, drawing at home; would not be cuddled or listen to stories, did not eat and did not sleep. He was like a little zombie.

The teacher said that John was backward and that the Child Guidance Clinic should be contacted. His mother panicked. Although it was obvious to her that John was not backward, she contacted Child Guidance Clinic because she was so worried about John's withdrawn behaviour. The headmistress was then upset because the family had contacted the Child Guidance. John should have been referred only through the school. Anyway, the headmistress told them to wait a while before doing anything with Child Guidance.

When the Head discovered after two terms what methods this frightening teacher was using to punish the children, a new teacher was appointed, but shortly afterwards John and his family had to move house, and this entailed a new school.

John was five years eight months when they moved house. He was frightened at night in the new home. It was one rather gloomy wing of a very large house which housed a museum and which was open to the public. The house was set in parkland. John had a wonderful time in the park that summer, enjoying meeting the visitors to the park and museum.

His new school was a small Church School with a caring staff. He started here in September. But, with the memory of his treatment in the previous school, he did not want to go. He was carried to school each morning by his mother, screaming, and then taken in by one of the staff, still crying. But when mother collected him at the end of the day he was reasonably settled. In the evening he would play happily in the park.

His panic began at bedtime. In the morning .....once more carrying a screaming child to school. By the time winter began, he suffered from diarrhoea every morning before school.

Before going to school having had no breakfast, he would now lie on the quarry tiled floor and beat his head on the floor. He did the same when he arrived back from school. He did not eat proper meals, only fruit and cheese etc., left around by mum.

The doctor said they should see a psychiatrist. It was the doctor's view that the trouble was caused by living in the gloomy old house. But at weekends and holidays John was quite happy and normal. It was obviously something about school. He was very happy when he went to visit his grandparents.

He saw a psychiatrist once a week for two years from the age of six. His parents were told at this time that he was slightly below normal in reading ability, but they found out years later that he had a reading age of seven years nine months when he was six, according to the psychiatrist's written report. Why had they been told an untruth?

He was not eating properly at home, only little titbits left around by mother, but she did not worry as he was staying at school for dinner. Then she was asked to send him to school with a packed lunch because his screams as the dinner-lady tried to force-feed him were disturbing the rest of the children! Long term food problems had been set up for the future by this treatment. Although his mother now sent him to school with a packed lunch, it remained uneaten.

At this time he also started being very upset if he had pen marks or plasticine on his hands. "They are dirty", he would say. His parents had never been the sort of people to worry about a bit of paint or clay on his clothes. Had something happened at school? The psychiatrist insisted it was a "guilt thing".

At this school the teaching was formal, in small groups, and he started writing little stories. This school reversed the idea of the previous school, that he was "backward". He had some difficulty with maths because he always knew the answer and wrote it down without showing the working. He got into trouble about this.

During this period he started to set himself maths problems at home. He discovered hundreds, tens and units for himself. At school he was told off for doing these as "they weren't ready to do them". The psychiatrist was furious and told the parents not to set John any sums at home. They hadn't. He had set them himself. The psychiatrist said "No child of six sets himself mathematical problems. He should be diverted into games like snakes and ladders". Now John cried because he was not allowed to do sums at home!

The psychiatrist said that it was living in the gloomy old house which caused all the trouble and recommended that John should go to hospital and attend the hospital school. (Psychiatric unit??) In other words, the child should be removed from his parents.

When the parents told the headteacher, he and the staff were horrified. They saw a sensitive, kind child who was extremely worried. John's parents refused to agree with this and withdrew him from Child Guidance.

During his sixth year, John wanted to play the recorder, but he was too young to start lessons at school. He learnt to play at home. After being shown the fingering by a relative, he taught himself, but was not allowed to join the school recorder class until he was seven; by this time he was reasonably proficient and had to join a class of complete beginners, which he found rather frustrating. He lost interest but stayed with the recorder group until he left the school at the age of nine. The teacher said he was the best recorder player in the whole school, but would not put him with the older ones because he was only seven years old.

At home, he learnt about the working of a wind-up gramophone, the workings of a bicycle, he read books on electronics, painted pictures, went hill walking. He was always busy, never bored, but still bothered about going to school.

They moved house again when John was nine years nine months. His new school was again a small Church School with a nice staff. The local children thought the whole family was "thick". (Northern accent and no car!). The staff and headmaster thought John was charming. The head said, "John has the best mind of any child I ever had in the school". He again played in the school recorder group.

His parents and the staff had thought that John would be at this school for two years, but then schooling was reorganized in the area and "middle schools" were set up so:-

John started a new school at age ten years nine months. He left the junior school with a glowing report, but things he was not interested in he just could not absorb.

Then the dreaded last nine years began.

When he started his new school he was, once more, silent with terror. The first day was a bad one. One of the other boys "borrowed" John's ink cartridges, broke them open, and used them for spreading drawings on the outside windows.

John was blamed because he had ink on his hands. He was too frightened to say he had not done it. (Several children, however, told the teacher that John was not the culprit)

The next day John was white and trembling. His mother went with him to explain that he had not been responsible for the ink episode. After this, each day was HELL: mother dragged a white and trembling child to school; the school secretary took him into her office and then had to get his teacher to help drag John into the classroom. He was taken, crying, to school every morning. Sometimes it would be as late as 9.30 by the time they arrived at school, as he had started having diarrhoea again. (Also nightmares and fear of going to sleep).

The theory was that if he were taken straight into class, he would "stop that noise" because he would be shamed by the other children.

His parents found out later that on many of these occasions he had been marked absent because he was not in the classroom at the time the register was marked.

During this time, one of the dinner ladies had followed John in the playground, asking questions like "Does your dad hit you?" "Does your mum hit you?." "Does your dad hit your mum", etc. When mother complained to the Head, he said this was the method often used to "find out what was wrong at home".

The secretary was on one occasion talking to a friend of John's mother. John was mentioned in the conversation. The friend said that she knew John. "Oh" said the secretary "we all know that that boy's problem is his mother".

(When a list of rude words was printed on the blackboard, again John was accused and again did not defend himself. He was also horrified if some other child were unjustly accused.)

His form teacher was kind but could not understand his fear. The sports teacher would have preferred that those who did not like football should be allowed some other form of activity instead, but he was not allowed to have his way. John wore glasses so he was always extra worried about the possibility of breaking his glasses during football.

John's father gave him some 16 mm film to run through his toy projector. John examined the film under the microscope and when he saw that it had a story on it he determined to make a machine to show the film. He planned it and worked it out himself, and finally had made a machine which worked on the principle of an old fashioned peep-show. At first his machine was worked by a handlever; later, by electricity or batteries.

At one time, the children had to prepare a talk on a subject which interested them. John was petrified, but his mother persuaded him to write a talk on toy projectors and his collection of Disney films, she helped to prepare his talk. When the day arrived, he was even more bothered than usual about going to school.

He arrived late and was catapulted directly into the English class and had to give his talk. He did not give his prepared talk about toy projectors. Instead he talked about the machine he had invented and made to show the 16 mm film. The teacher and pupils were captivated and he spoke for a whole hour instead of the half hour he had been asked to. The teacher could not understand how someone who could speak so lucidly about an invention could be such a duffer at comprehension. The teacher said that this was the only talk given by one of the children that had captured the attention of the whole class.

John was asked to bring the machine the next week. He also took that lesson, and the 30 children were excited, and loved watching the film. Even afterwards, the children called John "the professor" and his standing went up with them but NOT with the other teachers.

The Maths Teacher complained that John was always asking questions about aspects of maths that the class had not yet "done". He stopped asking questions and slowed down his learning practically to a stand-still.

The Music Teacher said he was a dud at music. (He had been the best recorder player in one of his previous schools).

The Home Economics Teacher accused him of not having done his meticulous homework. She said his mother had done it for him.

The Headmaster called Mrs Smith to his office one day and said that if she wouldn't insist on bringing John to school each day he would come quite happily by himself! The headmaster and secretary used to look out of the window, laughing, while mother dragged a screaming John to school, where he clung to the gatepost, white faced and shaking. Then the secretary would come out and drag the child into school.

John used to cook his own food at home and eat and eat. He became a compulsive eater and became overweight.

The French Teacher started ridiculing him about his weight and encouraged the children to do the same. One of the children told Mrs Smith that they did not do much French because they mostly talked and laughed about John's weight.

The Art Teacher and the **Craft Teacher**, however, were very nice.

Towards the end of the school year Mrs Smith went to the doctor. She had heard there was something called school phobia which seemed to explain all John's symptoms. The G.P. was scornful and gave John drugs: valium and tryptizol (amitryptiline) – tranquillizer and tricyclic antidepressant, taken simultaneously. These were supposed to dull the fear of school.

Sure enough, he did not cry the next week. He was a zombie. He spent every morning asleep in the sickroom, but the school did not mind. He was marked present in the attendance register. That was all they were interested in.

After one week, his parents took him off the drugs. They

didn't want a zombie for a son. Mother again went to the G.P. saying she had heard that there was a way of treating school phobics by keeping them at home for a month, a teacher coming in every day to give a lesson and gradually building up to returning to school. The G.P. was very angry, "You cannot have your son at home because you are lonely." The G.P. then said he would be informing the authorities.

Sure enough, Mrs Smith soon received a letter from the school psychiatrist saying that the G.P. had been in touch with her and that she believed that Mrs Smith had asked to see her. Mother wrote back to say no, she had not wished to see the psychiatrist. The psychiatrist replied that she was sorry that Mrs Smith would not see her, as she was sure she could help.

Also the Education Welfare Officer (truancy officer) called "to see if she could help."

All this worry and stress led to parents becoming impatient with John. This certainly helped no one, least of all John who was now losing trust in his parents.

His second year at this school began very badly. He had an unpleasant form mistress, the history teacher. John had to go in by the main school gates. How many times did they arrive after 9 a.m. when the gates were locked? Mother then had to find the secretary who had to find the caretaker to unlock the gates. She then left John at the gates. (Parents were not allowed beyond the gates).

Illness and Bereavement

John's beloved grandmother died. His mother went to the funeral, leaving John with his father. John was so upset that Mr Smith stayed from work for two days, and on the third day practically "carried" him to school, screaming.

John's form teacher called Mrs Smith on the phone and

invited her to a meeting about John. At the meeting, the form teacher said she thought he ought to go to a school where he could have remedial lessons for reading, etc. Mother tried to make her see that it was panic which made John unable to learn properly in her class – this particular teacher worried John a lot. (The English teacher who had been so impressed with John's invention had given him a reading test at age eleven – his ability, by this test, was thirteen years nine months).

At this point the family consulted the National Association for Gifted Children who arranged an I.Q. test. Although John did not do his best, because of panic, he scored 125; sufficient proof that he did not need remedial teaching. They could not put John in a school for "retarded" children.

Unfortunately, this appointment took place on the day that Nana died and he therefore felt guilty for Nana's death. Somehow it was confused in his mind with "causing trouble at school", and he felt that "if I had been good, she wouldn't have died." Consequently, for the rest of that year the situation became much worse and he would lie sobbing in the lane while mother tried vainly to move him to school. (Father helped getting him to school whenever he had a day off).

At this school the children were given "effort marks" and the headmaster called John's name out in assembly in front of the whole school, as "the boy who has the least number of effort marks in the whole school."

He got nil for P.E. and games. The punishment was to see how many times he could dress and undress in half an hour after school, every day for a week. One day he was forgotten and locked in. His mother waited for him outside school. She went home, he was not there. About an hour later he turned up in a shocked state. The caretaker had heard him knocking at the door. When Mrs Smith told the teacher next day, she just laughed.

After the day when John was shut in the sickroom all day with acute earache, they decided to look for a more understanding school.

Enquiries were made at the other middle school in the area. The headmaster was sympathetic and most of the staff were understanding and compassionate people, but the terror pattern had already set in and his parents continued forcing John to yet another school.

They struggled on in this way until the October half term.

After the October half term, Mr and Mrs Smith half carried a screaming child to school. They managed to get him into the sickroom, with the help of the school helper. He was white with fatigue. (He no longer slept at night. He would be stiff and frightened in the night, calling for his parents periodically). The school helper said she would keep an eye on him and take him to class when he had calmed down. She said she was "used to tantrums." Father and mother both tried to explain that this was no tantrum – it was panic. During the morning, mother phoned the school and the voice at the other end assured her that John was fine now.

At one o'clock John arrived home. His face was blank. He had no coat and it was pouring with rain. He said no word, went upstairs, lay down on his bed with all his wet clothes and his shoes, and went to sleep.

At three o'clock the phone rang, it was the EWO. "John is missing," she said. He had been left in the sick room and everyone had forgotten he was there. It was not until the end of the day, when his coat and bag were discovered in the sick room, that the helper remembered about him.

They belonged to National Association for Gifted Children (NAGC) at that time. John and his mother went to the Saturday activity group. (They found out that many of the children had been considered "backward" or "dull" by one or more of their teachers).

At this point they decided to educate John at home for a

short while, until he settled. Their hope was that as he became more settled, they would be able to gradually re-introduce him to school as they had heard had been done successfully with school phobic children, on a radio programme. *There should have been no difficulty.* Father has a degree in art and a *diploma of education.* They went to the Head and asked for work for John to do at home. This was refused. Anyway, John no longer enjoyed any structured work which smacked of school. Now he no longer even read books because he "had to read" at school.

They contacted the school psychology department saying what they intended to do. The educational psychologist came to see them in about three weeks time.

Meanwhile, every day John attempted school. Sometimes the Educational Welfare Officer came and took him. When this happened, he stayed until lunch time then came home and mother could not get him to go back.

When the EWO collected John, he was numb with fright and did not say a word. She remarked, "I don't know why he is so good with me when he isn't with you." She could not see that what she took to be "being good" was, in reality, abject fear.

When the educational psychologist came to see Mrs Smith he said there were "various methods" of dealing with school phobia but first of all it would be necessary for the whole family to see the child psychiatrist. Until this was arranged, he advised giving John some work at home until "something was sorted out."

So they started teaching him at home, impatiently waiting for the meeting with the child psychiatrist.

After three weeks the EWO came and said that if John was away for four weeks he would be taken into care!

Mother explained about the meeting with the educational psychologist and said they were waiting for the educational psychologist to contact them.

The EWO said she would take John to school. Mother said

they must wait for the psychiatrist to advise.

The next day the EWO arrived saying she had contacted the child psychiatrist who said she must take John to school. She took him for three days. He was in a state of shock; he did not talk, did not sleep, just ate and ate and ate.

The EWO phoned the next day to say that she was ill and the parents would have to force him to school. Mother and a friend took him to school in a car and he stayed all day.

Then came the beginning of the worst years of John's school life.

They were summoned to a meeting held in the psychiatry unit of the area schools' medical unit, some miles away.

It was not a meeting, it was a court martial. They had told John that when they saw the psychiatrist, he would be able to help him.

At the meeting: Psychiatrist: Dr H.

Social worker Mr M.

Assistant psychologist: Miss B.

EWO: Mrs A. and John with his father and mother.

Questions were fired thick and fast. Mother made a note of some of them.

Dr H. had mother in tears with his remarks about "keeping him at home to keep her company", etc.

Dr H. kept on turning to Mr M, Miss B. and Mrs A. saying, "Mrs Smith does not know what I am saying, doesn't understand, misunderstands me" etc.

The psychiatrist accused the father of "being against the system". He was furious. He works in it. He said, "Without the system we would starve".

They were being hammered about "expecting someone else to do what you should do, get your child to school."

The EWO said "I suspected trouble when John was at the

166

first middle school, but I didn't have enough evidence to make a case." The parents could not understand this, as mother had taken John to school every day under very difficult conditions. Then the truth came out. On the mornings when he had arrived in a very upset condition and spent time in the sickroom, he had been marked absent because he was not in the classroom when the register was called. So, many days he had been marked absent when he was in fact in school.

John was then told that he must go back to school or he would be taken into care, and to use the time at school to recover and not to learn. (Parents found this unbelievable)

John was asked what he thought of this. He said "The consequences don't seem very good, but I feel very bad about it, and I know I will have to go to school." He turned to his dad. "We are back to square one, aren't we, Dad". It was horrible. The psychologist, psychiatrist and EWO looked at each other and *smiled*.

The psychologist said, "We cannot help you in the way you want us to, but I can help you learn to read, John" and, to his parents, "I can help him with his reading"

(At the time of the 16 mm film talks, when there had been talk of John needing remedial reading, the teacher who organized the film had given John a reading test. He had thirteen years nine months ability at the age of eleven. The teacher who gave the test "couldn't understand Mrs S's (the form teacher's) fuss."

The following day, Mr Smith was late for work: a procedure which was to be kept up for years....... often resulting in great difficulties at the college where he taught. By the time they had forced John to school, he had to catch a train to college. Sometimes it was almost lunch-time when he arrived.

Mother rang the educational psychologist who had assessed John (NAGC). He suggested that they should go to their G.P. and ask for an appointment with a psychiatrist in

167

Great Ormond Street, which she did.

She rang the Head of the junior school who had been so supportive. He said "No court would take John away from from a caring home like yours."

The G.P. told Mr and Mrs Smith that Dr H. (the school psychiatrist) had said she was "unable to do anything to help because of the nature of the meeting" caused by them *"insisting that education was brought into it to complicate things."* However, he agreed to to refer to them to Great Ormond Street, but was unhelpful. *"This is an educational, not a medical problem."*

Mr Smith phoned the school's psychologist who came the following morning.

31st October 1978. John was 12 years old.

Mr F. the school's psychologist came. John was ready for school. Mr and Mrs Smith had told him that Mr F. was coming to talk to him about his fear of school, (that is what they had been told). Mr F. knocked at the door; Came in, said, "Right, John, I've come to take you to school". John screamed. Ran into the kitchen with Mr F. after him. He shut the door behind him and they stayed in there for almost two hours. Mr F. said "How long has this been going on .... seven and a half years? It's gone on too long." He suggested a home tutor, with a view to feeding John back to school the next year.

Mother took John to see psychiatrist and social worker at Great Ormond Street. She said, "John comes from a very happy and creative home. The trouble lies in school and the way he feels about it." She said he would not go back to school as the parents did not want him to. At the time, his parents thought this was an unfair comment but, in retrospect, it seems to them that she understood that they thought school was not right for him.

It was December 12th when a tutor was eventually found for John. She came to see John next day. She was a lovely person.

During the Spring term until half term 1979, John went to Mrs J's house for lessons, for two hours each morning. It was thought better for him not to be taught in his own house. At first, Mrs J. had to come and collect him. Later, mother took him to the bus stop where he got on the bus alone, and he returned home alone. Mother, was never able to get him to walk to the bus stop on his own "in case Mrs A. (EWO) sees me" or "a teacher".

As he became less worried, a small miracle occurred. He bloomed again! Mrs Smith's diary contains the following, "The happiest family period since John was at the small Church Primary School."

He thrived and was obviously so well, chasing round on his racing bike. "John is thriving on a one-to-one relationship – shows in his work and manner" – Diary.

After Easter it was decided by the psychologist and tutor to "feed him back into school gently." For half the term he was taught by Mrs J. in the school. Then he progressed to going to various classes for a short while. The staff were caring and concerned, and the Head was as helpful as he could possibly be.

After half term he started to go to school by himself, on his racing bike, coming home for a snack at lunch time, going back happily in the afternoon. (This was the only time in his school life that he went to school on his own). The tutor was overjoyed. She had never taught someone who was frightened of school before.

Everything was fine at this time, BUT:-

This was the last term at the middle school. He had to move to the upper school, which had 2000 pupils, in September.

The psychologist and tutor tried to persuade the Head to let Mrs J. help John to settle in the new school, but the Head refused this. The psychologist and the Head had a row in the office.

At the beginning of the new school year, his parents

walked John to school. He seemed quite calm, expecting it to be a repeat of the last school. Slowly, day by day, his newly found self-confidence disappeared. By the end of the first week, mother was into the routine of ringing up the school to say she could not get him there. One of the teachers would come and collect him, but they would not let Mrs J. do this.

By the time October came, John was being taken to school and left at the door. (Parents were not allowed into the school building). Then he would run and hide himself in the woods by the canal. His parents would search for him. The Year Head would search for him. Then he would be given all the work he had missed at school, plus his normal homework. He sobbed and cried and fell asleep.

Then a long round of sickness, diarrhoea, sleeplessness and weeping set in.

The teachers tried hard to help him. The games teacher taught him to swim. The physics teacher just talked to him during lessons as the work they were doing, John had done years ago at home. The physics teacher tried to get the Head to agree that John should do O-level physics that year, but the Head would not agree to this.

At half term, Mrs J., the tutor rang. She was angry at not being allowed to help John into upper school. She had been told, when she was employed to teach him, that part of her job was to "feed him" into upper school. She said that Mr B., the Year Head, preferred to handle the situation in his own way, which he did, with disastrous results.

The next months were a nightmare. They could never get John out of the house in the morning. When he eventually did go out, he would rush off to the woods, with his parents after him. Father was often late for work. There was trouble about this, of course.

They rang up Mr F., the Psychologist, who said he "would see John in school." John sobbed every day. One day he came home at break-time, took his bike and disappeared. He spent the day in a churchyard, among the gravestones.

Mrs J. rang. She had been all over the place looking for him.

Mr F. rang. He said he would do what he could to help but, because of government reorganization, he was not allowed to help over 13's who now had to be referred to the EWO as truant.

In November, Mr F. saw John in school. At this time he was being kept in every lunch time and playtime, to do work he missed when he ran away from school. On this occasion John arrived home in a shocked state, shaking violently. He had been talking to Mr F. who had been angry with him, then he had been teased in the playground and ran home.

Mrs Smith's diary, 31st October, "Don't know how to handle this. His confidence is lost. It seems to us that John is being treated as a truant. John longs for the Mrs J. days ....so do we".

Mr B. rang to say that he could no longer collect John to take him to school AND he wouldn't let Mrs J. bring him to school. Mrs J. rang, and explained that Mr F. was angry with the Year Head and had bitter rows with him.

The days became terrible. John was now taller than his mother. If John did not go to school, either the EWO or a teacher would come and take him. One morning, both John and his mother were crying and, for the first and only time, came to blows over going to school. Just at that moment, Mr B. came to collect him for school.

John was asked to help with the lighting for the school play. That should give him an interest in school and help to overcome his fears.

In November, mother had serious thrombophlebitis and the doctor (a new G.P.) wanted her to go into hospital. Mother refused, saying that she had to be at home with John. The doctor understood and came daily to treat the leg.

Mother had her bed downstairs, and had to stay in bed all

day. Meanwhile there was a continual procession of people in and out of the house. Mr Smith, John, EWO, teacher and of course, the doctor.

Father took John to school each morning, making himself late for college again. If John did not go to school or if he disappeared during the day, a teacher or EWO would come and collect him.

One day, on Mr Smith's day off, he took John to school three times.

On one occasion John came home at lunch time, sobbing and crying that he could not cope with school and could not go back. Suddenly, he remembered that there was a physics test. He wanted to do it, but it had started at 2 o'clock and he would be late for it. He went to school, by himself, to do the test. He did it in one hour instead of two and got 95%

The situation got worse. There was a parade of teachers and EWO in and out still, dragging him, shouting at him, blaming him for "causing people a lot of trouble" etc.

He worked hard on the school lighting, after school, but on weekends and in the evenings he found it impossible to go back to help with the lighting. Mother wrote to the English teacher to explain that they could not rely on John to help with any rehearsals, etc., outside school hours. The English teacher phoned that evening and said that they (the staff) had not realised "it was that bad". They had thought that by encouraging him out of lessons he would be able to face school in lessons.

John said that school was frightening because it was so BIG and so LONG.

The English teacher said they had had a meeting about John and was surprised that his parents were not there. He couldn't believe it when Mrs Smith said they had not been told about any meeting.

The EWO and psychologist said they were "making an arrangement" between themselves for a meeting with the parents. The EWO said "something must be done".

The EWO had been asking John "what is wrong with your home?" and "what sort of intelligence do you think you have?" John was puzzled. She also said, "Your parents won't love you if you don't go to school." Mother rang the EWO the next day to ask why she had said all this. She replied, "It's the truth. I've only told him the truth."

During this time, the physics teacher became interested in John's invention. He let John take it into lessons and talk to the children about it. They were most impressed. The physics teacher said that John "had done more in building it than most people do in a lifetime." John was perplexed by this because he had a very low self-image, and most of the teachers, it seemed, did not think much of him.

The EWO and psychologist were coming, to "see if they could arrange something." The family was unnerved by this and by the way the EWO had been talking to John.

The meeting took place in the Smith's home. Mr F. was pacing around shouting at Mrs A. The parents said they did get him to school, and that it caused them great pain to do so, as John was obviously so very frightened, and then he mostly came home at breaktime. Mr F. was furious and shouted at Mrs A. "Surely something can be done about that, for God's sake."

Then they suggested a hostel or residential school. The parents wanted a tutor again to help him back into school, as he had been helped before by Mrs J. (John had thrived on a one-to-one relationship). The officials said that John was far too intelligent to benefit from a tutor. His parents said that all John had ever learnt, he had learnt out of school.

The EWO told John that if his parents did not agree to residential school, he would be taken to court and taken into care.

Mother rang NAGC, (National Association for Gifted Children). The NAGC spokeswoman said they must not allow John to go to a school for naughty boys or a school for the sub-normal, which was often what happened in a case

173

like this.

The EWO called again. Mr Smith asked her why Mr F. (psychologist) thought a residential school would be good for John when he had told the parents he was "against it." She said "Get in touch with my superiors." This they did. They were referred back to Mr F.

They rang the school. The school staff wanted John to remain in the school, but the Education Department felt he should go to a residential school. The psychologist thought he should remain at his present school.

They rang John's ex-tutor, Mrs J. She said Mr F. did not want John to have a tutor because he was "so gifted."

On John's 14th birthday, they rang the Head of the Junior school. He said "Contact a solicitor." They went to the solicitor. He said they could not be taken to court for not allowing John to go to a "special school", but they could be fined for not sending him to school; there was no law which covered "school refusers".

They rang Mr F. who said sorry for the confusion, John was nothing to do with the Education Department.

On Dec 19th there was a meeting at school with John's form teacher, Head of Year and Deputy Head of Year. They all liked John and wanted to keep him.

The Christmas Holidays

This was the first Christmas that they had not gone to stay with relations. Mrs Smith had just started hobbling around, John was in a "het up" state, and Mr Smith felt ill so they decided to stay at home. On Dec. 31st, Mrs Smith's sister rang to say that her father had died. Once again, Mrs Smith went to a funeral, leaving John at home with his father for two days. John had now lost his beloved Grandfather.

When mother returned from the funeral, Mr Smith was bright yellow. He had contracted a virus and was ill for two months. John was in a state. His granny had died two years ago and now: mother had been ill for a long time, grandad had died, and now his Dad was ill – all in quick succession.

At the start of the new school term, panic and diarrhoea set in. They rang the school and Mr D. came to collect John. They told him about Grandad's death, etc. Every day, someone forced John to school, again.

A friend took John to school in a car, but he went missing as soon as he arrived.

John talked about boarding school. He said he knew it would be better for his parents. He didn't want to go. His parents didn't want him to go, either. (By now he had been brain-washed into believing that residential school would be best).

Mr Smith wrote to the Education office, asking for a tutor. John refused to go to school so Mr Smith set him some work to do at home.

The doctor gave John imipramine (tricyclic anti-depressant). They tried it once, only to give John a good night's sleep. He wouldn't get up in the morning. The EWO came.

The day Mr Smith went to hospital for tests, Mrs Smith went with him. John said he would go to school himself but of course he didn't.

The EWO came again. Mr Smith asked her if she had rung Mr F. but she replied, no. Mr F. was not involved any more as there was "nothing up with John."

During the Christmas Holidays, Mrs Smith gave her diaries of all their troubles to the solicitor. The solicitor said that parents are responsible for getting a child to school, and that school phobia is not recognised by the law.

John reacted very badly to his grandfather's death, and went about with a dazed look on his face. He was not sleeping, and was craving food at all times.

The teachers said, "He is alright in school" i.e. he is not a trouble maker (apart from running away and hiding in churchyards).

His parents said "he is grieving for his Grandad", but the teachers could not see that this was in any way a contributary factor. They said that he was worried about home. The parents said, "he is worried about school"

Everyday was HELL, trying to get him up and to school. (He was much bigger than his mother by now).

Now and again, he would manage a whole day at school, but mostly he would come home at mid-morning, or there would be a teacher or EWO at the door to say he was missing. Because his parents were enforcing his attendance at school, he now felt that they no longer loved him and were against him. He was unable to talk to anyone about his troubles. Sometimes he would be full of determination to go to school, but would freeze up at the door, or at the gate. By now he suffered quite severely from agoraphobia.

Mr Smith had now got into trouble about being late for work, so frequently it was left to mother alone to struggle and get him to school.

At the end of January, Mr Smith wrote to the education officer asking for a home tutor again.

John was distraught every day, but on Friday evening he started to relax. On Saturday he was relaxed, and then, on Sunday, he started to get in a state once more.

Mother enlisted the help of a friend again. Each day they both helped to get John into the car and took him to school. On most days, he slipped out of school between lessons, and disappeared for the rest of the day.

The education officer wrote offering John a place in a hostel for maladjusted boys, together with a place in the nearby school for disturbed children, or a tutor for two hours a day in *school*.

There was no way they would give him a tutor at home because of his age and ability; and by this time his parents did not think he would do any schoolwork at home; because, by now, he had the horrors of schoolwork.

Mother rang John's ex-tutor whose husband was a probation officer, to ask about the boy's hostel. Her husband was shocked, as the hostel was for boys who had been in trouble with the police: drugs, alcohol, vandalizing, fornicating and victimizing.

Mr Smith wrote to the education officer and accepted the tutor in school. The area tutor organizer came. She said he was "on a cushy number, frankly"..... and, "surely he can get there for two hours", and "I don't believe in mollycoddling children."

John said "Yes, I'll be there." He could not bring himself to tell the officials how he really felt.

The new tutor came to see John, told him that he must go to school on his own and his mother was not to take him.

On the following Monday morning, Mother could not get John out of the gate. He just stood there, shaking and sweating, rigid with fear. After struggling for some time, mother rang the school, but the tutor had already left. She then rang the supervisor who said she would come for him on the following morning, Tuesday, which she did. John spent two hours with the tutor in school.

On Tuesday evening, mother rang the supervisor, to ask if she was taking him the next day. The supervisor said she was not, and would mother promise that John would be in school. Mother replied that she could make no such promise as John was by now so much bigger than she was.

On Wednesday, mother could not get John out of the door, so she rang the school and was told that the tutor had not been seen. She then tried to ring the tutor at the school where she was based, but was not allowed to speak to her.

On Thursday, John would not, could not, move. He lay in bed absolutely rigid. So mother walked up to the school herself. The tutor was not there. She waited for a whole hour, but the tutor did not turn up.

Mother then returned home where John was in bed, in a terrified state. She then rang the tutor's school and was allowed to speak to her this time. The tutor said she had not been to John's school that morning or the day before, because her supervisor had told her not to turn up, as Mrs Smith had phoned to say she did not think she would be able to get him there.

Life then became a panic of solicitors, EWO and psychologist, etc.

The psychologist said John could not be taken into care because he had reported him as being school phobic;

The EWO said, "This is in higher hands;"

The Assistant Education officer said no one would take him into care because he had not been truanting.

The solicitor said it would not be possible, as they had not received Attendance Orders; and the school would not give him work to do at home, even though Mr Smith is a qualified teacher.

One day Mrs Smith received a phone call from Mr B., John's Year Head. He asked that Mr Smith should ring back immediately he arrived home from work. When Mr Smith phoned, he heard that there had been a meeting concerning John and the decision had been made to take him into care. Mr B. said, "If you can't get him to school, get him out of the area and into a boarding school."

They rang the Junior School Head who said,"No magistrate will take a child away from a good home and good parents like you." They rang the ex-tutor's husband, the probation officer. He was horrified. He told his wife that it was disgusting that children like John were treated like young criminals. He did not see how the authorities could get the family to court.

They rang the Head of the National Association for Gifted children. She said that they should get him into a private school, preferably out of the county; that there was no point in hiring a tutor at home, as they would still be answerable to the LEA.

The next morning they rang the solicitor and made an appointment for the afternoon. He said it would be impossible for the authorities to serve a care order when they had not given them Attendance Orders at any time. He was disgusted at the turn of events, but told them to get John into a private school out of the area.

They first went to visit a rather prim private school. John was petrified and like a zombie. It was obvious that, in his present state, he would be unable to cope with such a school.

Next they visited a Steiner school, and almost had to beg for them to take John. The staff were very reluctant to do this, as the whole Steiner principle is that the child should seek the school, and they were also reluctant to take on a problem.

When the family arrived home that evening, there were three large paper packets on the door mat. CARE ORDERS; one each for Mr Smith., Mrs Smith and John. The LEA was going to try and take him into care for the reason that they were not ALLOWING him to be educated according to his age and ability.

John was like a stunned creature. His parents had to undress him and get him to bed – only to get him up at 6 a.m. (He had not slept). Then they had to catch the 7.30 am train to the school. His parents had to literally drag him and push him from the station to the school. (Half an hour's walk at the best of times). Then Mr Smith had to run back to the station and catch the train to college. This went on for several weeks. There was more trouble at work because Mr Smith was not getting there on time. Then mother would rush round Estate Agents and solicitors, until it was time to collect John from school.

They kept going, in this fashion until the summer, and during this time sold their house (£3,000 off, for a quick sale), and bought a new house near the Steiner school, for £2,000 more than the much better house which they left behind.

They could not move until the end of September, so during September they were still forcing John up the road to the station, and from the station to the school at the other end.

Eventually they moved into their new house. The court had "stayed the case" for two months as John was now in school, but it was imperative that they move into their new house before October, otherwise they would all have to appear in court. In the event, the solicitor appeared for them. Of course he won, because he used Mrs Smith's diaries. The solicitor had told them that it was "the frighteners" that were being put on them, and that the LEA would be "laughed out of court."

By the time he reached school leaving age, he was agoraphobic, suicidal and unemployable. At the age of 19, he sat cringing in the corner as though he wanted to sink through the floor. By the time he was 20, he had recovered very slightly, so that he would go out of the house if his mother accompanied him.

If the measure of success is school attendance, then this is presumably a success story but, by using any other criteria, it is a disaster.

The boy will never be able to live a normal life unless some therapist somewhere can work a miracle. His parents feel their lives are shattered. Their health has been undermined. Mr Smith is permanently in a state of chronic depression, and Mrs Smith succumbs to numerous stress related illnesses.

For every 1000 school phobic children forced back to school by inhumane methods, there will be between 600 and 700 with similar stories.

Appendix to the story of John

John's depression continued for seven years after the official school leaving age. It was not until he was 23 that he managed to overcome it, and to move in a creative direction, a cheerful and happy person.

Unfortunately, this did not last, and he committed suicide at the age of 24.

CHAPTER TEN

Adults who have been Home Educated

Very few long-term studies have been carried out on the outcome of treatment for school phobia. Attendance at school is deemed to be success. This is a very short-term view. Long-term success I would take to be the development of the child into a balanced adult. Taking this long-term view, all the treatments provided by the schools' psychiatric teams are very poor.

According to the follow-up studies which have been carried out, school phobic children are likely to develop psychiatric trouble in later life.

Study 1

(D. Waller and L. Eisenberg in 'Out of school' edited by L. Hersov and I. Berg)

49 children	–	forced back to school
10 years later	–	13 were doing well.
	–	20 children showed definite limitations to developmental maturation and a "stifling of achievement
		14 children had severe psychiatric trouble (28% !!)
		50% were performing below expected level of ability
21 Years later	–	many of the children had developed into adults with a very limited and constricted life "continues to emphasize the consequent limitations to a rich,

full and varied life that have
ensued for many of the subjects."
–   **26% success.**

Study 2

(I. Berg in 'Out of school' edited by L. Hersov and I. Berg)
100 school phobic children were placed in a psychiatric unit
for seven months.
After only three years:-

$^1/_3$ had agoraphobia or severe psychiatric trouble
(six children had agoraphobia. nine others had
had further psychiatric treatment)
$^1/_3$ had mild neurotic trouble
Only $^1/_3$ were developing normally. **33% success.**

I would like to point out that in neither of these studies was
a control group used. In each case an equal number of
children educated at home, should have been used as a
control. A study of this kind, without a control, does not
demonstrate what the investigators say it does. It does not
show that school phobic children are likely to become
mentally unstable people. Instead, it suggests that forcing
school phobic children back to school by inhumane methods
is likely to cause mental problems in adult life.

In these two studies, only 26% and 33% respectively show
any signs of developing into balanced adults. This is
DISASTER.

The psychiatrists carrying out these investigations have
been so convinced that their approach was correct that, with
a complete disregard for scientific method, they ignored the
necessity for having a control and their results are therefore
experimentally invalid.

As a counterbalance to this research I am studying the

effect of home education on 100 school phobic children. Evidence which I have to date suggests that once the stress of school is removed, the children lose any neurotic tendencies such as a fear of people or agoraphobic tendencies, which they may have learnt in the school setting. At the time of writing (Oct, 1987), 13 children have completed three years following the school crisis and, I am happy to say, not one of them suffers from any mental trouble, though one of them (Derek) is still very nervous as a result of the severe harassment which he received at the hands of the "experts".

Footnote

By June 1989, 30 children had completed three years after the school crisis. There were no cases of mental illness, two were still afraid of people as a result of their experiences in school, and can be classed as neurotic.

Dick's mother writes:-

(This article first appeared in the Education Otherwise newsletter).

The letter dated 3rd May 1978 was to me the last straw. It was one in a long line of correspondence between myself and my son's headmaster. The sentence I really bridled at was, and I quote, "Perhaps it is time to seek medical or psychiatric explanation of his problem." That did it. Dick had needed no medical or psychiatric help on entering the comprehensive school two years earlier, after glowing references from his primary school headmaster, but two years and two terms of secondary education had reduced him to a pathetic shadow of his former self-confidence, who would indeed be seriously ill if the present unsatisfactory school situation continued. Already his nightmares were causing sleeplessness and loss of appetite which in turn caused over-tiredness and depression. I had been told some children manage the apparently hostile environment of the school with the help of tranquillizers. This knowledge appalled me and made me all the more determined to rescue Dick from his isolation and misery.

So just before his thirteenth birthday Dick was de-schooled. I wrote a final letter to the headmaster informing him that I was withdrawing my son. His brief reply told me that he would inform the local Chief Education Officer. I had taken much agonising to actually make this final decision and my husband, himself a teacher, was not wholly convinced that it was the right step to take. So many people, advisers, heads of department, welfare officers, etc., had all talked of failure if Dick left school. I insisted that to remain there with the aid of tranquillizers would, for me, also be defeat. The headmaster disagreed, telling me that many of his Rotary club friends kept going with the aid of tranquillizers and he admired them for it. I came away from that particular interview totally incredulous of their apparent lack of accountability and understanding. Three months after the interview the headmaster himself was suicidal and out of school for months. The other gent, the head of the lower school, collapsed of a heart attack eight days later. He had been a lifelong chain smoker. So, against the advice of these two highly socially successful gentlemen, I decided my son would stay at home and be given the chance to recover his previous enthusiasm for learning.

Because of his academic ability we had to agree with the Local Education Authority that he should continue his education with the view to sitting several "O" Level exams. We were told that advisers would visit us regularly to assess our son's progress. The visits were regular at first but later dropped off to a monthly check.

For the first few weeks after leaving school, Dick behaved much as a fugitive might, but gradually he regained his former appetite and vigour, although sleeplessness remained a problem because school nightmares still punctuated his sleep. However as the actual fear of school hostilities had been removed, the improvement to his general health was soon noticeable. When people asked me why Dick was out of school, I could always sum it up quite briefly by saying he was bright, bullied and bored. They needed no further explanation.

To get Dick to "O" Level standard we bought correspondence courses in seven subjects which made up a good spread of academic disciplines. Dick worked out his own timetables which really amounted to dividing the time before the exams by the number of lessons, then heading each lesson with what he called the "do by" date. This seemed to work very well and the advisers had to be satisfied with it as a timetable. Anyone taking a child out of school or considering it soon realises two things. Firstly the authorities have an obsession for written work, curriculum and timetables. In their opinion if a child is not committing words to paper, it is not learning. This attitude has become one of the biggest bugbears for many parents teaching their children at home. Secondly there is nothing, absolutely nothing wrong with the system. It is your child that is at fault. In my case the many letters I received from the authorities told me that Dick was just holding on to his mother's apron strings, he was lacking in self-reliance and unable to take advantage of the dynamic atmosphere of a busy comprehensive – and so on and so forth. Re-reading these old letters that caused so much pain at the time is now an amusing experience.

The biggest difficulty to overcome was fear of failure. This was a hangover from school where endless tests and numerical standards were devised to enable the children to compare success and failure, with of course bouquets for the successful and brick bats for the failures. I found the best way to help him was to take off the pressure by repeatedly explaining that if he did not pass his O' levels at the first sitting, there would be other opportunities to take them or alternatively simply to find work which did not require O'levels. The attitude always calmed him so I used it whenever he started to fret. Having lost his chance to compare himself with others seemed to undermine his confidence. However after having listened to a few radio programmes of "Top of the Form" his confidence returned because he was able to answer nearly all the questions, even those put to the eighteen year olds.

In June 1981 Dick sat seven O'levels at our local technical college as an external examinee. When the exams were over he felt he had passed them all quite easily. All that remained was to wait and see how good his grades would be. The day of the results dawned and not wishing to wait any longer than need be, he cycled to the college to collect his grades. To his delight he found he had gained all grade A's which, for the uninitiated, means top grade. He telephoned me immediately and I experienced one of the best moments of my life. Our success was all the sweeter because of all the cynicism and scepticism endured for so long.

Now I feel that the three and a half years that my son spent at home have benefitted all the family. We see all the results of the experiment which allowed him to study quietly at his own pace in his own way whilst not being subjected to the endless time-wasting practises of school. Time that otherwise would have been wasted during those vital years of development were spent exploring the environment and pursuing his many interests and hobbies which included astronomy, photography, including developing and printing, electronics, aero modelling, cycling and much more, wherever his curiosity took him. His knowledge of current affairs, national and worldwide became a source of incredulity to my husband who as a secondary school teacher, was well aware of most teenagers' ignorance in this area. This knowledge was acquired by the simple experience of listening to BBC Radio's "World at One". And I can verify that he did not have to write one word of it down to remember it. He went to the local technical college to study for A levels, which he passed with flying colours and was accepted by King's College, Cambridge.

His years of being separated from his peer group have not impared his ability to mix. He joins in with many sport and social activities, has arranged a college disco, represented the college in cross country races and become chairman of the full-time students' association.

For Dick there are never enough hours in the day to pursue all his interests and keep abreast of his academic work. The biggest bonus of taking him out of school has been never to have heard the words "I'm bored", pass his lips.

Now my only regret is that I ever let any of my three children go to school. I believe that the unnatural environment of a school produces neurotic behaviour. This behaviour takes the form of continual approval-seeking of peers and this type of behaviour kills independence and self love. Conformity is the name of the game. Its reward is never having to take a risk. Now, with the benefit of hindsight, all three of my children declare that their children will not be forced to attend school. I look forward to the prospect of delightful, life loving and neurosis free grandchildren.

Nora

Nora left school in 1954 – two years before the theory of "separation anxiety" was developed, therefore she was not harassed.

On the first day at infant school, she was knocked down in the playground by three older boys and she went home.

She was extremely unhappy at school. For several years after starting school she used to vomit in the morning. She stayed away from school on many occasions because of this.

Because she was so unhappy in the state primary school she was eventually sent to a small private school for two or three years, from whence she passed to the grammar school.

At first she enjoyed all the new subjects especially biology, but then the biology teacher who had made the subject so interesting was asked to leave. (She was not sticking to the syllabus).

After about 18 months, Nora felt she was in prison. She was still interested in the subjects, but the personalities of some of the teachers made it difficult for her to learn. (They were demanding, sarcastic, over-strict, bad tempered, fond of humiliating children and prone to throwing the board duster).

She enjoyed exams. In an exam she was actually doing something, instead of having something "done" to her. She went to school on exam days!

Once the first year at Grammar School was over, she was so unhappy that on many days she did not go to school. On the days she did attend, she was too unhappy to learn anything. She became a compulsive eater for a time. On average, she attended school about two days a week, and towards the end, it became much less than that.

Her time at home was not spent idling. She read avidly, some of it the work she should have done in school, kept a detailed nature diary, wrote her own stories, poetry etc., obedience trained her dog and went for long walks.

Nora left school officially at fifteen and a half.

She is now widowed with one child who is educated out of school.

Tom

Shortly after the move to secondary school Tom started vomiting every morning before school. He was frequently away from school because of his sickness.

The school attendance officer called and told mother that she must send him to school even though he vomited.

The next day, Tom caught the school bus. At half past nine mother received a telephone call "Please come and collect your son. He is vomiting". Mother is a busy farmer's wife. She was not pleased to have to leave the farm and drive the twelve miles to the (nearest) comprehensive school, to collect her son. After that he stayed at home, helping Dad on the farm.

190

When the school attendance officer called to say that he should be in school, mother replied, "My son's health is more important than his education." Fortunately for her, the official accepted this.

By the time he reached school leaving age he had a good practical grounding in farming. He then went to the local technical college to study an agricultural course.

He is now married with two children, and works as an agricultural contractor.

Once children who are troubled by school attendance have been told that it is possible to be taught at home, the healing process begins. The mere mention that it is not necessary to go to school, that the work can be done at home, relieves the pressure and stress to such an extent that some parents report improvement in their child's well being even before home education actually begins.

These children are highly motivated to work well at home because they know that failure to do so will lead to them being returned to the school system.

Some children after perhaps 12 or 18 months at home, decide they would like to return to school, others prefer to remain at home until they reach school-leaving age.

"But they will never learn to socialise," the cry is heard. Since many of the children have become school refusers precisely because of a fear of the very large numbers of people in our modern comprehensive schools, or because of fear of individual children, bullies, it is unlikely that they would have learned to socialise in that environment. In fact, our very large schools are probably the root cause of many people developing a social phobia in a crowd situation.

Any parent who is willing to educate a child out of school will be glad to take on the responsibilities of ensuring that the child will have adequate opportunities for socialisation.

CONCLUSION

Thomas Szasz in his book, 'The Myth of Mental Illness', compares the fate of people with mental illness with the fate of witches in mediaeval times. His contention is that mental illness occurs only because of the inability of a person to adapt to a specific social environment; that without the social context, mental illness ceases to exist and that without the constricted expectations of social convention, such people would rarely be classed as ill. Mental illness results from forcing square pegs into round holes.

The hounding of school phobic children by the authorities is certainly very reminiscent of a witch hunt. As with the witch hunt, the weak are hounded by the powerful; the people in the position of power, the psychiatrists, have their theories and will not listen to the explanations of their victims, just as the priests in mediaeval times would not listen to the protestations of innocence from so-called witches.

In follow-up studies of children with school phobia there has been no control group of children who were home educated. A follow-up study of such a nature proves nothing without a control. The follow-up studies which have been carried out are very disturbing: the results of treatment being that 60% or 70% of the children grew up to be adults prone to psychiatric problems.

The adults who have written to me, having been home-educated following a crisis, have grown up free from mental illness; the children who have been through great troubles and who have subsequently been educated at home, show every sign of developing normally, reverting to their normal cheerful selves when the stress of school is removed, though in some cases, the improvement is only very gradual and occurs over a period of several months.

Family tensions which have been high at the time of the school crisis, diminish and disappear as the whole family

192

involves itself in home education, which can be therapeutic, not only for the troubled child but for the whole family.

It is my belief that a policy of non-intervention in these cases would have a far more beneficial effect on the future life of these children than any of the enforced treatments, that have been carried out in the past 30 years.

The provision of a small grant for the family, towards home education, would be a far cheaper proposition than the expensive methods of treatment used now. The children would probably have a much better chance of developing into balanced adults.

But the children are the victims, in a weak and oppressed position.

Who would be the losers under such a regime? It would be the people in a position of power, the psychiatrists. If grants were no longer available to finance the treatment of many children in Child Guidance Clinics and psychiatric units, the powerful would be the losers. It is in their interests, therefore, to maintain the status quo, and thus to maintain their own status.

The educational system is meant to provide education in accordance with the wishes of their parents; but when parents have protested that they wish to teach their child at home, their requests have very often been ignored because of the psychiatrists' beliefs that their theories are correct; that the children should be separated from their parents. As the results from the follow-up studies show that, after treatment, over 60% of the children grow up to be adults prone to mental illness, who could be blamed for thinking the treatment useless?

In a largely literate society, it should be possible for virtually all school phobic children to be educated at home under the supervision of their parents. Every parent of a school phobic child should be given the option to do this. Of course there will be the possibility that there will be a very few families where this will encourage over-dependance on parents; but I think that most parents, given the challenge to educate their own child, will feel responsible for making sure the child has adequate opportunities for learning to socialise, and the risk of creating a few over-dependent children is a risk worth taking.

The option of educating a child out of school should also be given to the parents of truant children. I am convinced that very many parents would prefer to educate their children at home rather than to be hounded by the authorities, taken to court, and lose their children through care orders and residential school. Some of these families would need help in order to cope with educating their child, but I am sure that with such help, even families who are at present labelled "problem families" would be able to function at a higher level.

If we are given the freedom, encouragement and support to educate our children at home at the first sign of any disturbance at school, instead of allowing it to progress to the stage of mental breakdown or suicidal depression, there would be more chance that the children, after a period of being educated out of school, should want to return to school.

There are some very good schools. We should do all in our power to raise the standards, both academic and social, in the poorer schools; and we should be prepared to learn from all that is best in the educational systems of other countries.

Some changes are required:-

A.   Home Education

Parents who so wish, should be allowed to educate their children out of school, with no harassment. If a child becomes either school phobic or truant ("maladjusted" even), the possibility of home tuition under supervision of the parents should always be considered. The option of "otherwise" education should be more widely known. All parents should be given this information during their child's pre-school years, so that if the child shows signs of stress on entering school, the parents may decide to withdraw the child from school at least for a time, and educate him or her out of school until such time as he or she develops more confidence.

There should be a legal obligation upon the Local Education Authority to inform the parents of any child who does not attend school, either truant or school phobic, of the right to educate a child out of school. Both the 1944 Education Act and the 1969 Children and Young Persons Act should be amended so that it becomes the duty of Education Authorities to inform parents of any child who does not attend school, of their right to home education, before any threats are made, or action taken, to remove a child from his or her home into care, residential school or psychiatric unit; and before psychoactive drugs are used in order to enforce school attendance.

B.   Schools

i). The school entry age should be raised, belatedly following the recommendation of the Plowden Report (1967). For children to enter school at a more mature age than at present would be a tremendous improvement. Five year olds need to relate to a mother-figure. This is virtually impossible in an infant class with approximately 30 children per teacher.

The raising of the school entry age, with the simultaneous provision of an adequate number of optional kindergarten/playgroups, with a ratio of adult to child of about 1:8 is essential, especially in the areas designated as socially deprived.

Dr David Weikart's valuable study of the effects of pre-school nursery schools on the lives of disadvantaged children, with its careful follow-up study over a period of 20 years has shown conclusively that child-centred nursery schooling is valuable for later educational and social development. The type of programme followed in such a nursery school is extremely important as the "behaviourist" method had, according to his study, a disastrous social effect, which became evident only when the children reached adolescence.

Although many children are ready and eager for the wider environment of nursery school by the age of three, I have letters from several parents who say that long-term school problems were set in train by nursery school or playgroup and that their children had gone to nursery school before they were ready for this move. The workers in the nursery school/playgroup should be aware of this, and suggest to the parent of any child who seems to be unable to enjoy the situation, that she takes the child home, and waits until the child is older before bringing him or her back again.

ii). The present policy of herding children over the age of eleven into enormous, depersonalised schools has a dehumanising effect. This, together with other socially acceptable evils such as the cult of the peer group and the consequent split society (see Urie Bronfenbrenner – 'Two Worlds of Childhood') has helped to produce the alienated teenager, with consequences such as drug abuse and the increase in delinquency.

A tiny minority of children in this situation have mental breakdown or become suicidal. These children, the hyper-sensitive ones, act as a pointer, indicating that here is a stressful situation. Instead of victimizing and scapegoating these children, the pointer should be heeded, and moves made to create a less stressful environment. All children would benefit from this.

In his book 'Disaffection From School', Ken Reid states that 10% of school children are truant, 25% are neurotic and

13% maladjusted. This is a massive 48% of school children.

The object of education is presumably to produce well-balanced adults who can cope with the complexities of life. It seems that our schooling system is failing on the first, and ultimately most important, objective.

The fact that almost 50% of school children attain adulthood as disturbed or neurotic people is far more serious than any mere academic failure. It is a social disaster.

From an economic point of view it has grave implications, as a large number of these people will grow up with tendencies towards mental illness or delinquency, and will be a burden on the state.

They will also tend to transmit these tendencies onto their own children, creating yet another generation of neurotic and maladjusted people.

It is an indictment of our society that so many people grow up to become adults with a need for tranquillizers. Our schools are too big. Our children have spent far too much of their formative years in a stressful situation. There are various ways of decreasing school size. One such is as follows:-

Instead of one enormous school with 1,000 pupils, there could be five or more schools, each with 200 or fewer children. At the time of change from primary to secondary schooling (not necessarily at the same age as at present) it should be the children's choice which school they attend. There could be schools specialising in science, languages, the humanities, art, music, sport, crafts; ranging from an academic to a non-academic approach.

To say that a school specialises in, for instance, science is not to say that other subjects are ignored, but that there would be less time spent on them. I can imagine that a child interested in science would enjoy having long periods of science and short periods of French, whereas a child interested in languages would have the very reverse.

Children who are truant at present might well be happy to

go to school if they knew that the whole of each afternoon would be devoted to craft, sport or whatever. Under such a scheme, I believe the incidence of truancy would drop.

The growth point in education at the present time appears to be the provision of special schools for maladjusted children. If we ceased to force our children into such an abnormal environment as an enormous institution, it is my belief that far fewer children would be labelled as "maladjusted".

iii). **Choice.** In Britain at the present time there is very little choice in education. It is a case of one rule for the rich and another for everyone else.

The choice of private schools is available for those who can pay for them. There is also a government grant available for very bright children to go to a private school but, unless the school is geographically close to the child's home, this is only available to children whose parents can afford the boarding fees.

Apart from this very limited choice, there are only a very few small alternative schools such as The White Lion Street Free School, London, and The Small School in Devon.

If groups of parents and teachers were given grants to set up small schools, as in Denmark, new schools would be formed and they would provide much-needed choice.

Even to educate a child "otherwise" than at school costs money. Books, etc. must be purchased; some families whose children have been eligible for free school meals find that the extra food bill is significant. Families who have educated children over the age of 16 have discovered that they lose the Child Benefit. (This anomaly is, happily, ending; as the Government amend the Child Benefit Act in 1986).

iv). Another scheme, which would entail abandoning many of our preconceived notions of syllabus, curriculum and examination, would be to reorganize our education so that it becomes predominantly a character-building exercise.

Consider the Duke of Edinburgh's Award. This award is

aimed at building character. To attain this award, young people have to carry out various activities, including a skill, a physical activity, a community service and an expedition. It gives them opportunities to explore things they could find challenging, and to follow them through to a recognised level of achievement. Dedication, commitment and stamina are qualities that are developed by working for this award. The rewards and challenges which the young people meet in attaining these goals are of inestimable value in their development.

Reorganization of our schools, abandoning traditional curricula, and replacing traditional syllabus with a variety of projects which can be carried out by pupils, of their own choice and at their own rate, and leading to awards of different kinds, could have an enormous effect on the next generation of adults in our society.

A pilot scheme run on these lines could be initiated in one of the failing schools in the inner-city areas of deprivation, decay and unrest, which have been troubled by riots in the 1980's. To make use of necessary resources for such a scheme, schools would need to become informal resource centres, and would function in collaboration with swimming pools, sports centres and community services of various kinds: nursery schools, old people's homes, etc.

Unfortunately, I think it is unlikely that such a project would receive government approval, although it would probably have repercussions as diverse as a reduction in the numbers of truants and maladjusted children; and a lowering of the population of both prisons and mental hospitals.

C.   Schools Psychiatric Services

If a child develops a nervous breakdown, suicidal depression, or other sign of extreme stress, it should be acceptable for parents to care for their child at home with a minimum of external intervention, unless requested.

When a child is treated by the psychiatric personnel, the child's version of the circumstances leading up to the breakdown, should be believed. If a child, or his or her family, insist that it was bullying or intimidation which led to the build-up of intolerable stress, this fact should be treated with respect by the psychiatrist or psychologist, instead of their deciding that the child is afraid of parting from mother.

Social Factors Predisposing Towards Alienation of Teenagers

Our society is fragmented.

Due partly to the Industrial Revolution which removed the workplace from the home to a centralised factory; and partly to the mobility given to people by the aeroplane, the railways and the motor car, many families in this country tend to consist of one male adult who goes out to paid employment, and one female adult who cares for children and also does the many jobs around the house. The extended family as a neighbourhood phenomenon tends no longer to exist, as, owing to the mobility, families tend to live apart from their relatives.

As a result, children, in their earliest and most formative years, are brought up in an environment which is particularly barren of human material. In this environment, both the mother and the children are isolated from other adults. It is not good for the children, who have few adults whom they can observe and use as models for adult life, and a play area at home which can be boring, due to the fact that mother, the only adult around, often busies herself with housework instead of playing with her child, interacting with him or her and encouraging creative activity. (I am not blaming mother. Everything, from the Victorian dictum "cleanliness is next to Godliness" to the TV adverts for house cleaners, encourages the young mother to believe that having a spotless home is more important that interacting with her children).

Neither is this situation good for the mother who is isolated and overwhelmed with both jobs, of looking after the housework and meals, and of childcare; many women also have paid employment in addition to these two jobs. In most cases, the paid employment is seen as an economic essential. In other cases, it is used by the mother as an escape from the barren isolation.

This situation could be changed for the next generation if at least a fortnight's time, or preferably a longer period, spent helping in a children's pre-school playgroup became an essential part of all children's education, both boys and girls. In this way they would learn to react with small children and would hopefully be able to create a less barren environment for their own children.

Elizabeth Janeway in 'Between Myth and Morning' thinks that never before in history has the young mother with small children been so isolated, that, before the rise of rapid and easy transport, it was usual for people to live in a community where other members of the extended family, if not living in the same house, lived not far away. Such a society, with a number of adults with whom to inter-relate, was more interesting for the growing child, as well as being more supportive of the mother.

Onto an already split society, split into small isolated nuclear families, our schooling system has imposed another split. The school system, as we have it, has segregated children by age. This has resulted in the cult of the peer group. Children, to escape from the emotionally barren environment of the nuclear family have virtually no option but to gather together with those of their own age. The anti-social peer group has been accepted by psychiatrists, psychologists and the general public as being the normal way to develop. In his prophetic book 'Two Worlds of Childhood' written in the 1960's, Urie Bronfenbrenner foretells the breakdown of society and the increase in crime and delinquency which we are in fact witnessing in the mid 1980's. The author expected this breakdown to happen as a result of the two factors: the split into isolated nuclear families, and the age-segregation of the peer group, encouraged by the nature of our schooling system. (He also implicates television violence as a contributory factor in social breakdown. Although the television companies deny this, television is moulding our children's minds. The violence and crime on our television screens is absorbed by our children and echoed in many of their lives).

"Of course you have to go to school. Everyone has to go to school. Anyway, it's the law." How many children have had this reply when they have made a complaint to their parents about school? If a child is deeply distressed by any aspect of school, and receives a reply like this from his or her parents, communication breaks down. Is this the beginning of the "generation gap" in many families? The time when teenagers start locking themselves away in their bedrooms, away from other members of the family; the time of the rise of sulleness and rudeness?

If an individual family decides, for various reasons, to educate a child out of school, this is a small, individual move towards ending the alienation between one generation and the next. It should be encouraged, rather than the opposite.

If parents felt free to say, "Would you prefer to do your schoolwork at home?" fewer families would experience a split between one generation and the next.

Since the 1950's in this country it has been Government policy to replace the previously existing three-tier system of secondary schools with comprehensive schools. In theory, this has been to give all children an equal chance, educationally. Combined with this altruistic idea is the belief that all such schools should be big. The whole country is dotted with enormous schools to which children converge in buses each day. Bullying on the buses is rife. The driver is too busy driving the bus to control any bullying. I know of one occasion when the driver, in order to stop the bullying, left the girl who was being bullied at the side of the road and continued with all the bullies on the bus.

Many of the schools number 1000 pupils and some have as many as 2000. In such an atmosphere, it is impossible for any one person to know more than a small proportion of the people, individually. There is a breakdown in communication between people. Children become alienated. Some withdraw into their own teenage gang, which may be aggressive and bullying in nature. Others withdraw into themselves, become isolated and perhaps school phobic.

It should come as no surprise that shortly after forcing children into such a de-humanising environment, the twin problems of truancy and school phobia should become more common.

The problem of underachieving children is now so acute that it has become a government concern. This, also, can be a form of withdrawal from a stressful situation. (See 'Living with Stress' – Consumer's Association).

It is not the fact of comprehensive schools, as such, which causes these problems, and others such as delinquency. It is the de-humanising effect of placing children in such a vast crowd of people, where meaningful human relationships break down. It is not surprising that in such a situation teachers suffer from nervous breakdown. Neither should it surprise us that children suffer in this way.

Schools create an environment for the institutionalization of our children and, therefore, for the institutionalization of society, creating a society which is led by a bureaucratic machine, an illusion of true democracy.

Our schools are too big. They have become training grounds where people learn to become, in the words of R.D. Laing, "specks of crowd dust".

We can maintain the comprehensive ideal, and yet make

203

a move towards smaller schools. One possible way of doing this I have put forward in this book. There are others.

It is a pity that so much money has gone into the building of these enormous institutions, but money spent in replacing them with smaller schools will be money well spent, if it results in a reduction of human unhappiness and a reduction of social unrest.

The younger generation is accused of becoming alienated and aggressive but, given their environment, this is not surprising.

Bibliography

Chapter 1

Truancy and school absenteeism – Ken Reid – Hodder and Stoughton – 1985

Fact and fiction in psychology – H.J. Eysenck – Pelican – 1965

Phobias – Joy Melville – Unwin pubs. – 1979

Chapter 2

Out of school – L. Hersov and I. Berg et al. – Wiley – 1981

Sense and nonsense in psychology – H.J. Eysenck – Pelican – 1957

Childhood suicide behaviour – R. Kosky – J. Child psychol. psychiat., vol 24 No. 3 – 1983.

Right from the start – Selma Greenberg – Victor Gollancz – 1979

Youth and the social order – Frank Musgrove – Routledge and Kegan Paul – 1964

Two worlds of childhood, USSR and USA – Urie Bronfenbrenner – George Allen and Unwin – 1971

Chapter 3

Urie Bronfenbrenner – as above.

Selma Greenberg – as above.

Chapter 4

Living with stress – Consumer's Association – Hodder – 1982

Dealing with depression – Kathy Nairne and Gerrilyn Smith – Women's Press – 1984

Bonds of depression – G. Parker – Angus and Robertson – 1978

Depression after childbirth – Katherine Dalton – Oxford University Press – 1980.

Anorexia nervosa – P. Dally and J. Gomez – Heinemann – 1979.

Catherine – Maureen Dunbar – Viking – 1986

Chapter 5

L.Hersov and I.Berg et al. – as above.

Unwillingly to school – J. Kahn, J. Nurston, H. Carol Pergamon Press – 1975.

Consequences of three pre-school curriculum models through age 15 – Lawrence Schweinhart, David Weikart and Mary Larner – Early Childhood Development Quarterly – April 1986.

The Myth of the Hyperactive Child – P. Schrag and D. Divorky – Pelican – 1975.

The heart of the race – B. Bryan, S. Dadzie and S. Scafe – Virago Press – 1985.

Dictionary of Drugs – Richard Fisher and George Christie – Paladin – 1971.

Young Children In Action – M. Hohmann, B. Banet and David Weikart – High/Scope Educ. Research Foundation, Ypsilanti, Michigan, USA – 1979

Development Of Secure Units In Child Care – G.J. Blumental – Gower Publishing Co. – 1985

Chapter 7

A Last Resort? – Peter Newall – Penguin – 1972.

Disturbance in parent-child relationship following pre-term delivery – J.A. Jeffcoate, M.E. Humphrey and J.K. Lloyd – Develop. Med. Child Neurology. 1979 21.

The modern practice of separating a newborn baby from its mother. – D.H. Garrow and Diana Smith. – Proc. Roy. Soc. Med. volume 69 Jan 1976

Suicide and attempted suicide – Erwin Stengel – Pelican – 1964.

Childhood suicide behaviour – Kosky – as above.

Attempted suicide in children and adolescents – Keith Hawton – J. Child psychol. psychiat. Vol. 23 No. 4.

Adolescent disturbance and breakdown – Moses Laufer – Penguin – 1975.

Politics of Experience – R.D. Laing – Pelican – 1967

Psychoanalytic "Evidence" – A Critique Based on Freud's Case of Little Hans – Joseph Wolpe and Stanley Rachman – J. of Nervous and Mental Diseases – 1960 – p. 130-148

The Myth of Women's Masochism – Paula Caplan – Methuen – 1986

Suicide and Attempted Suicide Among Children and Adolescents – Keith Hawton – Sage Publications – 1986

Decline and Fall of the Freudian Empire – H.J. Eysenck – Pelican – 1986

The Assault on Truth: Freud's Suppression of the Seduction Theory – Jeffrey Masson – Farrar, Strauss and Giroux, USA – 1984

The Negative Scream: The Story of Young People Who Took an Overdose – Sally O'Brien – Routledge and Kegan Paul – 1985

Critical Essays In Psychoanalysis – ed. Stanley Rachman – Pergmon Press – 1963

Chapter 10

L. Hersov and I. Berg et al. – as above.

Conclusion

The myth of mental illness – Thomas Szasz – Harper and Row – 1984

Between Myth and Morning – Elizabeth Janeway –

Between Myth and Morning – Elizabeth Janeway – William Morrow and Co. New York – 1974

Living With Stress – as above.

Disaffection from School – Ken Reid – Methuen – 1986

General

Absent from school – Rob Grunsel – Writers and Readers Publishing Co-operative Ltd. – 1980

Escape from childhood – John Holt – Pelican – 1975.

Teach your own – John Holt – Lighthouse Books – 1981.

School and the Social Order – Ivan Illich – Penguin – 1979

School's Out: Educating Your Child at Home – Jean Bendall – Ashgrove Press – 1987